Right
The Book

CHANGING THE SCRIPT OF YOUR LIFE

Right The Book

Book

Changing The Script Of Your Life

Your Life Is A Drama That GOD Is Watching

By

Tiffany Kameni

Right the Book
Changing the Script of Your Life

Written by Tiffany Buckner-Kameni
Edited by Iris L. Jones
Proofread by B. Davinia Gordon
Layout by Anointed Fire Christian Publishing (Tiffany Kameni)
All Graphics and Illustrations by Tiffany Kameni

All scriptures were taken from the King James Version of the Bible unless otherwise indicated.

Contact Information
Tiffany Buckner-Kameni
info@anointedfire.com

Website:
www.tiffanykameni.com
www.anointedfire.com

Published by Anointed Fire Christian Publishing
www.anointedfirecp.com

ISBN-13:
978-0-9891579-0-2

ISBN-10:
0989157903

Dedication

I dedicate this book to the author and finisher of my faith: JEHOVAH

Dear FATHER,
You truly are my everything, and I love you more than life itself. Thank you for entrusting me to do everything you have placed in my hands and heart to do. I intend to glorify your mighty Name in everything and to not go one day without giving you the glory. You have stood by me through the worst and the best of times, and you have brought me through and revealed yourself to my heart each time. I love you and adore you, and I want to spend every waking moment of my life telling you and showing you how much I love you. I say it again; you are my everything. You are my bread, my breath, the light of my eyes and my peace as I rest. How can I not glorify you? You took a woman who was filthy, cleaned her up and chose to use her for your glory. You have proven yourself to me time and time again and now; I am at your feet saying "yes" to your will always.

FATHER, please take this book and use it for your glory and not my own. Glorify your Name and open the eyes and understanding of each reader so that everything you have written on my heart to share may be understood.

Precious FATHER, please place your loving hands on everyone who reads this book so that they can embrace a new chapter in their lives. Let this book not be fruitless, but let it yield much fruit for your Kingdom and your glory.

Glorify your Name, beautiful and wonderful GOD; Alpha and Omega; the Beginning and the End. Precious and Almighty El Shaddai, arrest every spirit that may attempt to stand in the way of understanding and bind every demon of distraction. Perfect and wonderful receiver of my soul, let this book continue to go forth even after my time in this earth expires. Let this book continue to live on and bless your people.

Once again, FATHER; glorify your Name.

In the name of CHRIST JESUS I pray,
Amen.

Introduction

Welcome to the first day of a changed you.

Do you ever feel like there is more to you that you don't know about yet? Do you want to explore who you are more, but you are unsure where to start? Who is this powerful character on the other side of you whose voice overrides the dimensions of time to call you outside of the comforts of familiarity? We are usually barricaded by three things: the fear of failure, the fear of success, and the fear of the unknown, therefore, we learn to accept our stories as they are. Sure, you want to finally become the strong man or woman of GOD that the Bible has told stories about, but it appears to be too complicated of a feat, but it's not.

I wrote 'Right The Book,' to help the readers see their lives from a story-telling point of view. When we see ourselves from a different angle, it is easier to welcome change. Our lives won't change, no matter how much we want them to, until our minds change. Giving the mind a reason to change never seems to be enough of an incentive to motivate us, something extra is needed. We need new information and we need to better understand who we are, where we are going and that the journey there won't kill us.

'Right The Book' gives us a GOD'S eye view of our lives and how it reads to GOD. Your life is a book that is being read by the ALMIGHTY GOD, and you are writing in this book every day. Every word that you speak is a pen stroke and every choice that you make has a coma behind it, meaning a consequence or blessing comes to finish off the sentence. When you "right" the book, you are simply saying no to adding more chapters of confusion, bitterness, anger, failure and any other wrong that has co-starred with you in your life's story. To "right" the book is to make a u-turn in the now and decide that you will not go any further where you are, but you will follow GOD, no matter what the price is.

Each chapter demonstrates the power of choices, words and

associations as they relate to your life's story as it is being read by GOD. Imagine if you had a house near a mountain, and you knew that you needed to get a new roof, but you kept putting it off. One day, you go for a hike in the mountains, and you can see your roof from the top of the mountain. It looks like it's about to cave in, so there will be no more waiting. You're now determined and motivated to go straight home and begin the repairs. 'Right The Book' is that mountain top view of your life that will help you to see yourself from another angle, so that you will welcome the repairs that GOD wants to make in your heart.

This book is a powerful, educational, and motivational tool that will change the way you look at life. Let's start reading! It only gets great from here!

Table of Contents

YOUR INTRODUCTION

Your introduction to this world was made on the day you were born. You were delivered into a wicked place as an innocent being. During your stay here, you were required to have a name, so your parents gave you a name. Your name is the identification of the character you are. Your name, in the earthly realm, is not necessarily your name in the spiritual realm, but it is simply used for others to identify you in the earth.

Your birth signified a change in the story for your parents as well. You were the beginning of a new chapter in their lives, and they had to learn to be more careful as to what they said and did. Maybe your dad finally decided to get serious and get a job to take care of you, or perhaps your dad decided that he wanted no part of your life, so he did everything to avoid you. However, this doesn't void the fact that his life was forever changed at that moment because he now knew that he had a son or daughter out there, and he had to live with the fact that he was a deadbeat dad. Whether he cared or not, his life was changed.

Maybe your mom finally decided to stop partying and concentrate more on getting an education, so she could be a better provider for you; or maybe she viewed her children as a complication and decided not to be that mother we all need to start off our lives on the right note.

No matter how they were then or how they are now, when you became an adult, you began to write your own story, but as a baby, you were in their books, and they started to write chapters about your life. Some of those chapters were great and maybe some of them were awful. What your parents added to your life has started the book. Nevertheless, you have the pencil to decide now how it reads and how it ends.

Our introduction is our starting point, and many have had some pretty bad starts. However, our beginning does not determine how our story ends; it only gives GOD more of an opportunity to glorify HIS name. For example, let's say you were born to parents who lived in poverty, an abusive dad, an alcoholic mother, and you were abused as a child. Statistics say you are doomed to become an alcoholic, be an abuser or be in abusive relationships and live in poverty. However, if you would dare to let the WORD of GOD change your life and your mind, you will put many to shame and many statistics to rest.

Think about your life. How did your story begin? Were you born to a two-parent household or were you born to a single mother? People who have had the worst starts have the greatest opportunities because when we are low, we have to be launched with greater force to get us out of our pits. Therefore, we need to put that "born with a silver spoon in one's mouth" adage to rest. A man or a woman who was born in a life of lack, brokenness and rejection will feel the impact of his downtime; however, he will grow immune to these things and get the wisdom in these things. So, he has a great opportunity (if he takes it) to grab a hold of the greatest wealth that man could ever find, and that wealth is wisdom. He knows how to be poor, survive and still keep a smile on his face. But, most men who are not accustomed to struggling cannot survive should their wealth leave them.

So, again, in your story, you can find plenty of reasons to throw yourself a pity party, but wisdom has her own party going on. If you are not feasting with wisdom, you are going to nibble on foolishness and have to continue throwing pity parties for yourself and your friends.

<u>YOUR ACKNOWLEDGMENT</u>

Many authors take the time out to acknowledge the people who have helped them with the publishing, set up, and distribution of their books, and this is done on the acknowledgment page of the book.

For your life, there are many people who are unknowingly on your acknowledgment page because there are many who have contributed to the success or failure of your life. Your parents, for example, are usually the first set of faces that you recognize and acknowledge. As we grow older and more mature in CHRIST, however, we learn to acknowledge GOD first because HE is Supreme. The people who have taught us how strong we are in CHRIST were the people who hurt us the most.

Let's say that you have a friend, and he has been by your side for years. One day, you discover that he stole your wallet and all of your money in it. You call the police, have him arrested and continue on in life without him. Then, you find out a little later that he had been hitting on your 14-year-old daughter the whole time he'd been hanging around you. Later, you remember an incident where $500 had gone missing from your office desk, but you thought your wife's brother was the sticky-fingered bandit because he had been over visiting that day. The list keeps adding up, and the hard truth comes rolling in; this guy wasn't your friend; he was a friendly enemy! So, you are extremely careful nowadays about the people you let near your family, and you've learned not to leave loose cash around your house. You may tell others that he did you wrong, and he did, but he also came in and taught you a few things; therefore, in your life's story, he will have his own acknowledgment.

The people we consider friendly and helpful have played roles in our stories, and they undoubtedly are listed in our acknowledgments, but the people who played the greatest roles in our stories were the not-so-friendly and helpful ones! One of the stories I hear often (especially amongst those with prophetic gifts or Prophets) are the stories of first being mishandled by a parent or both parents. The parent had a favorite child and bestowed all of their love and attention on that child, but for the storyteller, they were usually left to fend for themselves. They grew up feeling unloved and tried to figure out why their parent or parents chose to mishandle them. The truth is, a natural man or woman; even as a parent, cannot recognize or understand the behaviors of a man or woman of GOD in training; especially one that's anointed! In most of these cases, the doted upon child grows up and lives a disappointing life; but the child left to his or her own devices, grows up to be strong, GOD-fearing and successful. When talking with these characters, many of them recognize that their success is partly due to the fact that they learned how to deal with hardship at such a young age. Few of them recognize; however, that GOD designed them to stand in the enemy's territory and come out as the victorious one. Their first hurts were simply their first training courses; and as vigorous as they were, they were beneficial. Therefore, the child who was smothered with love would be able to acknowledge his or her parents in a sentence because their stories don't usually read well, but the child who was neglected could dedicate a whole book to their parent or parents because they were the first defensive-living obstacles that they had to get around.

Our lives are full of characters who played roles in our stories; many of them deserving a place in the acknowledgment section, while others were simply extras or behind-the-scenes characters. Your enemies are often times more deserving of an acknowledgment than your friends because they didn't just help you to make a decision, but they pushed you into a praying position.

YOUR TABLE OF CONTENTS

Your table of contents is a list of any and every event that has occurred in your life. If we could dress up our books for the LORD, we'd probably place heart-shaped drawings near the chapters, we loved the most and sad faces near the ones we hated. Nevertheless, every chapter in your life leads to the next chapter.

Again, GOD has given you the pen and called you the author of your destiny while CHRIST is the author and finisher of your faith (*See Hebrews 12:2*). You can choose how Chapter 1 of your life (your today) affects Chapter 2 of your life (your tomorrow) by making Chapter 1 a story worth reading in the ears of the LORD. What you do today will determine what scenes will play out for you tomorrow; therefore, your story is a scene by scene cast of choices and consequences. Even now, before the book is completed, you have already placed your life's chapters in your table of contents to be added to later. Maybe you plan to go to college; maybe you plan to get married, or maybe you're planning to "go off" on a particular person the next time you see them. Right now, you are setting your life's chapters up and determining how they will read to the LORD.

Often times, we cry and complain about the direction of our lives, but in truth, no one has the pen to write in your life what you haven't allowed them to write. Mother, father, sister, brother, friend, enemy....it doesn't matter. When you became an adult, you had the pen to write your life out for GOD to read and no one else could force you to let them write on your lives, unless they took your pen away by force. Whoever you hand that pen to is going to write on your life, whether they write good things or bad things; they will write something. Let's go back to the alcoholic dad, for example. Sure, you love him and you wish that he'd change, but is he changing? Why complain that he's taking you through heartache when you can take your pen out of his hand? The problem with a lot of people is that they feel obligated to let people write in their lives just because these people are related to them, has helped them out before, or has been there for them at some point. We have been trained to believe that others have the right to publish negative chapters in our lives because they have a title in our hearts; when in truth, you have to be willing to walk away from poisonous relationships if you desire to live in peace. In staying, you can't complain when they pick up the pen and smear ink all over you; you can't complain when the next chapter they write is one of them talking about you, ridiculing you or trying to bring you down. Anyone you allow into your life, you have handed them a pen to write on your life; and they have the right to use it because you gave it to them.

Think about Abraham and Lot. If you've read any of my books, you will see that I love to use Abraham and Lot as an example because their story has fed me over and over again. When Lot's herdsmen began to have strife with Abraham's herdsmen, Abraham basically asked Lot to depart from him. He didn't stop loving Lot; he didn't turn his back on Lot; he simply asked Lot to go his own way. Why was that? Because Abraham understood that a negative sentence had been written, and that sentence was going to spin off into a story that would bring him out of the blessed zone.

Again, that's the problem with most people; they often times don't know when to separate from one another in love. Abraham was taking control of his life's book, and he wasn't going to let even a paragraph of strife be completed. Notice that it's a short story about the strife between the herdsmen. Abraham didn't let it climb up to come between him and his nephew; he diffused the problem before it became a problem. But, our strife stories are usually very long. We tolerate people for years, decades and even lifetimes that should have been gone a long time ago. If you knew how much you were paying for these people to stay in your life, you would pay them top dollar to separate from you.

However, it's your book; you will choose how the table of contents line up. Today is setting you up for the next chapter in your life, and if you choose sin; you give death, disease, destruction and poverty the right to write on your life. Many souls have chosen fornication, for example, and their next chapter begins with what disease they were diagnosed with or the pregnancy and birth of a child to a one-parent household. So that baby's chapter is set up with a table of contents that includes heartbreak over the absence of one parent. Yes, your book does affect the chapters in the lives of others; namely, your children or your children to come.

Then, you still have to deal with the WORD of GOD; which won't return to the LORD void.
When HE calls something sin, and HE has decreed judgment upon it, it is done! When you go out there and participate in a sinful act, judgment comes and populates your book. Your book may read, for example:
Chapter 1: Committing Adultery With Walter
Chapter 2: Getting Tired of My Husband
Chapter 3: The Chastening
Chapter 4: Where Did My Finances Go?
Chapter 5: The Divorce Proceedings
Chapter 6: Walter Was a Loser; He Left Me

Do you see how the chapters lined up to tell the story? Consequence always has the right to write on your life and everything birthed in sin delivers a consequence.

GOD has already set up our table of contents. HE has plans for us, but in our sinful hearts, we devise plans that we feel are better suited for ourselves, and we erase those chapters that GOD has commanded us to live in. GOD gave us the right to do this when HE gave us free will. HIS plans for you and I are to bless us, but Satan is so crafty that he has managed to convince the people of GOD that there is an alternative to GOD'S way. So, we head off into sin, looking for that blessing that Satan said was hidden in the depths of darkness. Indeed, it sounds crazy once you hear it or see it written out. How can one go into sin trying to find a blessing? But, we do it and come out with consequence as one of our co-authors, and then we complain that we don't like what consequence is writing.

Are you tired of the way your book is reading? Do you want to change what's in it? It starts with the chapters. Look into your heart and review the chapters you have written, and if you don't like the way they read, don't write another chapter that begins or ends in sin. Look into your imagination and pay attention to the chapters you are planning for your life. Do they involve the LORD or did you add HIM as a prop for your story to make it sound righteous? When your life is all about you, you will have some chapters that are going to start and end in misery. You shouldn't create chapters; instead, you should walk in the chapters that GOD has spelled out for you and populate those chapters with righteousness. When they start off right, they end up righteous.

Think about this: Theresa is making one of her favorite stews. Against her husband's advice; she takes 10 jalapeno peppers, cuts them up and places them in the stew. When the stew is ready, Theresa takes one bite and starts to complain about her stew being too spicy. She is furious with her husband because she says that it is his fault. Had he not said that it would be too spicy, that stew would have been perfect! Is Theresa's husband to blame for the super spicy stew? Of course not! Theresa used an excessive amount of peppers and as a result; her stew was spicy.

Isn't this what we do to the LORD? HE says not to do something, and we do it anyway. Then consequence comes in and takes its place, and that's when people start crying out to GOD and rebuking the devil; not wanting to understand that consequence won't be moved with their words. It isn't there to attack a righteous man or woman; it is there to collect the debt that a sinner created. That's when folks get mad at GOD and want to know why HE let the enemy attack them, but it isn't HIS fault that they chose sin. HE warned us all beforehand about the wages of sin; therefore, if you head into it anyway; you are in the same saying that you can handle what sin deposits into your life.

It's your life; you will decide how you want your book to read. Right now, you have already set up a table of contents for your life, and it is up to you to cancel your plans and fall back into GOD'S will for your life. Sure, many of the chapters that GOD has written out for us will include some challenges. Nevertheless, how you handle those challenges will determine how the story ends and how the next chapter begins. While we are living in this earth, we will come face-to-face with trials; but wisdom will teach you that a trial is an opportunity for you to declare yourself innocent when Satan is trying to convict you of wrongdoing. In your obedience to the WORD, you will not only be declared innocent, but you can come back and sue the enemy for wrongfully accusing you and for false imprisonment. There is wealth in those challenges! There is wisdom there! Of course, we want to live in "happily ever after" at all times, but even fairy tales involve a challenge and an overcoming; that's how it works. You are challenged, and you overcome by the Blood of the Lamb.

Let's change some of the chapters in your table of contents. You say that you want to please the LORD, own businesses, have a GOD-fearing and successful family and be healthy. Your table of contents should read:

Chapter 1: Repentance
Chapter 2: Finding My Way Back to GOD
Chapter 3: Rejecting Who I Was to Embrace Who I Am
Chapter 4: Leading By Example
Chapter 5: Praying For Guidance in Life and in Business
Chapter 6: Researching Business Advice
Chapter 7: Investing in What GOD Has Given Me
Chapter 8: Launching My Business
Chapter 9: Advertising and Waiting
Chapter 10: Continuing in the LORD
Chapter 11: Refusing to Give Up
Chapter 12: Letting Go of Hindrances

You can go on and on to include your family and more ideas for your life. Draw up a time-line. If you want to start a business, for example; what's your time-line to do this? If you don't have one, you haven't added it to your book just yet. You're just thinking about adding that chapter to your life, but thinking about something and actually doing it are as different as night and day.

Right the Book

Go into your heart and remove all of the negative chapters you have already added to your table of contents. This is where you are going to predetermine and re-determine how your life goes and how it reads to GOD. The most important thing about your life's journey is that it reads in a way that makes the LORD want to add blessings to your story.

THE CHARACTERS IN YOUR STORY

Everyone who comes into your life is a character in your story. Now, some people have minor roles because they are simply passing through. You may even get by without noticing them, but many of them have been penciled in as a part of your story, and they will have some small effect on a sentence, paragraph or chapter in your life. A great example would be that time your car broke down in the middle of the road, and a stranger stopped to help you out. You may not have remembered his name, but one day; you are riding along, and you see someone on the side of the road. Their car has broken down, and your heart goes out to them, so you may have stopped because you can now relate to how they feel, and you want to see how you can offer them a helping hand. Or maybe you saw the person who helped you out in the supermarket. They were standing in line trying to figure out why their debit card is being denied. Recognizing them, you happily tell the cashier to add their groceries to your ticket. As minor as they seemed, they did play a role in your life's story. They added more character to your character. It's funny; sometimes we can remember good Samaritans a lot more than we can remember short-lived friendships because that Samaritan touched your heart in a special way.

Everyone you meet is auditioning to play a part in your story, and they want you to have a part in their story. That's why you have to pray about everyone who enters your life so that you can know what role they are auditioning for and what role they are recruiting you for. Everyone who comes into your story brings their own pencils, and they can and will write on your life. You may get indignant when you don't like what they are writing, but the truth of the matter is: they still play a part in your story, whether they were called by GOD to you or sent by the enemy.

Then, of course, there is family. Again, most people think that family has the right to write on their lives, so they allow people to weigh them down and keep them down for their stay here on Earth simply because they are related in the natural. But, how did JESUS view family? Mark 3:31-35 demonstrates the views of CHRIST. ***"There came then his brethren and his mother, and, standing without, sent unto him, calling him. And the multitude sat about him, and they said unto him, Behold, thy mother and thy brethren without seek for thee. And he answered them, saying, Who is my mother, or my brethren? And he looked round about on them which sat about him, and said, Behold my mother and my brethren! For whosoever shall do the will of God, the same is my brother, and my sister, and mother."***

JESUS was casting away the perceived importance of the natural family to help us to understand the true importance of the spiritual family. When you give yourself to CHRIST, you are no longer related to the people in your natural family who don't have a relationship with HIM. Your goal in their lives is to tell them about CHRIST. When they make it clear they don't want HIM, but they want the old dead you; you are not to resurrect the unsaved character that you were to feed their sinful hearts! Instead, you have to disassociate yourself from them, or they will bring you back down to your daily grave until sin has marked a permanent spot for you. Guaranteed!

One of the greatest travesties to hit the modern-day Christian is the belief that we owe someone something. Satan is crafty indeed! Someone comes along while you are yet in your sin, and they help you out. Maybe they gave you a car, or maybe they hugged you when you were crying. Whatever they did; you now feel like you owe them. The problem is, they have never tried to collect this mental debt, or you've paid them back over and over again; but you still feel indebted to them. So, you're now saved and they are still in the world, but you keep going around them, sowing into their lives and participating in their wickedness because you feel that you owe them. ***"Owe no man anything, but to love one another: for he that loves another has fulfilled the law" (Romans 13:8).***

In your indebted thinking, you have made yourself their slave, and you are now serving this mindset, and they will cash in on it because they don't understand the things or the heart of GOD. To them, you owe them, and they will remind you of this should you ever come out of line. Didn't GOD give HIS only-begotten Son to die for your sins? Didn't GOD give you another day to live and another breath to breathe? So, why is it that we have trouble seeing what we owe GOD, but we are always indebted to one another?

Nevertheless, you keep them around anyway, and you keep paying them back over and over again with your very soul. When trials and tribulations meet you where you stand, you want to get mad at the LORD and act as if HE owes you something. You have erected these people as characters in your story and not just any character; they carry on the essence of a god because you are serving them and ignoring the wishes of the only true and living GOD. Sure, you come to church, and you may even pay your tithes, but without obedience; it's all for nothing! The greatest act of worship does not come from your lips; it comes from your life.

There are characters who GOD placed in your life to be a part of your story, and there are characters that the enemy placed into your life to change the way your story reads. You have the right to determine how far each character gets in your life. Often times, we allow the wrong characters in because they present this plot to us that sounds so good that we want to be a part of it. However, once they were in your life, they wrote a different message than that of what you thought they'd write. Now, you're angry, hurt and telling the world how you've been betrayed; but you weren't betrayed by them. We only betray ourselves when we believe every word that drips from the mouth of a man when GOD has already declared in Romans 3:4, **"Let GOD be true and every man a liar."** GOD also told you to try the spirit by the spirit to see if it is of GOD, but you didn't do that. (*See 1 John 4:1*) Instead, you believed what they said, and you gave them a chapter in your life, and they broke out the crayons and started scribbling all over your life. They weren't supposed to be there; therefore, they didn't know the value of your life. In other words, they weren't mature enough to write in your life; therefore, they played with your life.

Again, every character that comes into your life will write on your life, or they may rewrite your entire life's script. We often live in hope; hoping that our life's characters are genuine, and they won't do the wrong things, but GOD has called us to live in faith. We should know HIS WORD and have faith in HIS WORD so that when we come in contact with our Sauls, we will know not to dine with them or when we meet our Lots, we will know when the time comes to separate from them. No man should have a greater place in your heart than GOD. Never. Not even your children.

Then, there are the romantic relationships. These are the relationships that will impact your story the greatest because they often times involve sex and soul ties. Don't misunderstand because all relationships birth soul ties, but having a sexual relationship with a person is one of the greatest soul ties around because the two shall become one. (*See Mark 10:8*) There will be many who come along and want the role of being your girlfriend, boyfriend, wife, husband, or bedroom buddy. GOD warned us about fornication because fornication creates some chapters in your life that will have some of the most gut-wrenching, heart-breaking, tear-jerking scenes you could have ever witnessed. Soul ties are not easy to break, and they don't just go away when you get tired of a person. A soul tie has to be divided by GOD, and it is done when you have repented of the sin and decided to walk in righteousness. You can't go to the LORD in fornication and ask HIM to sever your soul tie with Charlie because you are now with Danny, and you want to be for Danny only. To repent is to turn away from the sin entirely.

Ladies, when a man comes into your life, and he wants to engage sexually with you; he is asking to become your illegal husband, but there's a problem with this script. A husband absolutely has to cover his wife because a woman is not to be opened without a covering. A wife will long for her husband because she was created from his rib, but when a man comes in illegally, opens her up and doesn't cover her; her head is exposed to devils. Now, this is a completely different book, but I'll try to explain it. A woman was created to be the wife of one man and when she marries this man, she will become his wife through intercourse; not by ritual. Yes, we have the wedding ceremonies, but they are traditional acts of man instated by man for man, but when a husband took a wife in the Bible, he simply asked her father for her, and he went in unto her. You'd probably say, "No, that's fornication!" But, it's not. When she was a virgin, and he lay with her, he became her husband, and he was supposed to carry on the duties of a husband. Those duties included taking care of her, birthing children with her and taking care of those children. That's why in the Biblical days, the men of GOD went after women of GOD, but they asked the dads for their daughter's hands in marriage. After he approved them, they didn't have a wedding ceremony; the husband took her and lay with her and afterward; they had a reception. Her dad was her covering until her husband came along. It is the same nowadays; your FATHER in heaven is your covering through your obedience until your husband comes along bearing the CHRIST head as his covering. GOD continues to cover you through your husband after your marriage. Your husband has to ask your heavenly FATHER for your hand in marriage, and then he has to honor man's law (*See Mark 12:17*) by going before a judge or a priest to declare his new role and accept the responsibilities of this new role before man and GOD.

Review the story of Amnon and Tamar. Amnon was David's son and he was in love with his sister, Tamar. Now, in those days, it wasn't a bad thing for them to marry because the Jews had to intermarry within their own to keep from polluting themselves with the Gentiles. Anyhow, Amnon set his sister up by pretending to be sick. He told David to send Tamar in to feed him, and David did. When Tamar came in, Amnon raped her. Before the rape, Tamar pleaded with him and told him to simply ask David for her hand, and she said that without a doubt, David would not withhold her from Amnon. Amnon didn't listen to her, but instead, he raped her and after the rape, the Bible tells us that he hated Tamar greater than he had previously loved her, and he told her to get up and leave. Tamar's response shows how wicked of an act her brother had just committed by refusing to cover her as a husband and sending her away instead. *"And she said unto him, There is no cause: this evil in sending me away is greater than the other that thou didst unto me" (2 Samuel 13:16).*

Ladies: When you allow a man to enter, and he sends you away; he sends you away exposed and, often times, what he previously felt for you will, like a puff of smoke, disappear. But, your heart will still be in the relationship because his soul is now one with your soul. He has made a deposit and as such; he is now the husband; a major character in your life and he will play a major part in how your future relationships play out. Therefore, even when he leaves your life, he still has a pen to write on your life. Your story starts to sound like: I saw John today at the park, and he was looking great. He was walking with his average looking-girlfriend, and I just had to make myself seen. So, I walked ahead of them, making sure that I strutted my stuff in their face. After all, I look better than her, right? Can someone answer that question? Anyhow, when I left the park, I couldn't get him out of my head, so I called him and he hung up on me. How could he reject me for her? Look at me! Now, look at her! Who looks better?

This is pure, uncensored foolishness, and it is now written in someone's life because they chose to bring the wrong man in and then have the nerves to try and intimidate any woman they saw him with. Maybe his girlfriend is his GOD appointed wife and then again, maybe she's just another woman who got lost in her own wishes and took on the wrong man. But, now, she has a pen along with him, to write on your life. What's the story going to read? That you got into a fight with a woman over a man who didn't want you? Are you not ashamed to publish that?

Stay away from lust! It does not lead to love, nor does it bring in the blessings you so desire. Sure, your favorite celebrity might have had a baby out of wedlock and ended up marrying this beautiful, successful man and now; you're hyped up. You can't wait to find or be found by your handsome hunk of a millionaire, so you wait and wait. Meanwhile, GOD sees your heart, and HE wouldn't dare send your husband to you because you'd reject him. You want devils covered in beautiful skin and a full set of teeth. You have to understand that any man you bring into your life and into your bedroom is going to start a chapter in your life that you can't erase. Is it going to read that this man became the father of your children and then walked away? You expected him to be a "man" and stick around for those children, but you never expected him to be a "husband" and stick around to cover you. Can you see how this looks to GOD? And that man did what you expected; he gave you a part of himself and walked away. He was a 'man'. He was a 'real man', but he was not a man of GOD and he never assumed the responsibility of a husband. There is a difference.

Gentlemen: Anytime you have sex with a woman, you are basically saying to GOD that you are going to take on the role and the responsibility of a husband. When you lie with her, you are affirming this and when you abandon her, you are saying to GOD that HIS will is not your will, and that you will do as you please. So, you leave her open and exposed to devils. I understand that she submitted herself to you, and most men would lie with her, but if you are a man of GOD; you should have ministered to her and not touched her like a husband. When you decide to not cover her as a husband, but to uncover her nakedness, you bring the wrath of GOD upon yourself. Every time she cries out to GOD in need; your name comes up before the LORD as the man who had vowed (through sex) to take care of her. (That is unless she has lain with another man since she lain with you.)

I understand that your flesh cries out for sex, but you have to understand that wisdom cries out in the marketplace for those who want wisdom to come in and feast on what she has to offer. When you choose to lie with a woman instead of utilizing that time to feast on wisdom, you are choosing the consequences of being a stray husband. Your relationships to the women you want don't work out for you because your soul has been deposited into many women, and they are crying out. Yes, even the men of GOD had multiple wives, but they took care of them. Therefore, if you are going to act like a husband, you have to act like a husband wholly. You have to provide for the woman whom you uncovered.

Now, you see the woman you once pretended to love out walking with another man, and this jealousy arises in you. Why is that? You don't love her, so why are you jealous over her? Because you are one of her husbands! *"And the spirit of jealousy come upon him, and he be jealous of his wife, and she be defiled: or if the spirit of jealousy come upon him, and he be jealous of his wife, and she be not defiled...."* *(Numbers 5:14)*

Every woman you meet will write a chapter in your life, and you will write one in hers. If you lie with her and walk away, you will walk away hindered, especially if her tears arise before the LORD. *"Likewise, ye husbands, dwell with them according to knowledge, giving honour unto the wife, as unto the weaker vessel, and as being heirs together of the grace of life; that your prayers be not hindered"* *(1 Peter 3:7).*

When you walk away from a woman after lying with her, you become her husband, and when you don't honor the WORD of the LORD to dwell with her, honor her as the weaker vessel and live as an heir with her, your prayers are hindered. The only way you are released from this is if she was to go out and sleep with another man, and you put her away with a divorce. (Note: Man cannot separate a union, only GOD can; therefore, a divorce will be to repent and ask GOD to separate the union.) Because she is your wife, and you are her husband; you can't put her away. *"And I say unto you, Whosoever shall put away his wife, except it be for fornication, and shall marry another, committeth adultery: and whoso marrieth her which is put away doth commit adultery"* *(Matthew 19:9).*

Your choices today are writing chapters in your life. What about that loose woman who left you to be with another man?

What should you do? Again, Matthew 19:9 reflects your release. You are free to move forward (after repentance) because she chose to take another man in and let him act as her husband. Repent and live in your freedom, especially if you laid with her without marrying her in the eyes of the LORD. That doesn't mean a traditional ceremony, but to make a commitment to the LORD to serve your role as husband in her life and to cover her with the covering of CHRIST that you are commanded to walk under. Should you have a ceremony? Yes, because the Bible tells us to honor the laws of the land. The law says you need a ceremony before the law recognizes you as husband and wife, and we often times get this confused with what GOD sees. HE sees you as one person with the women with whom you have slept with; not just the woman with whom you had a traditional marriage ceremony.

Ladies and Gentlemen: When you act as a spouse, GOD will treat you as a spouse. Don't get mad and spiteful at the people who have lain with you and walked away. You were the one who gave them this pen, and you understood that this pen did not have an eraser. You made a choice, and you chose to dishonor the WORD of GOD to honor your own wishes. Know that every relationship you get into will write on your life. Every man or woman you sleep with will have a chapter in your book. And the worst part is, GOD reads from this book, and HE endures the heartbreak of every detail of your relationships. When HIS WORD responds to your relationships and your choices, there is no need for tears. Believe it or not, even when you say "yes" to a man or "yes" to a woman, GOD can come along and override your "yes" with a "no," and you just have to deal with it. Of course, HE is protecting you and your anointing. Nevertheless; it still hurts when you have set your mind and your heart to believing that a person is going to be with you until the end of time.

As for past relationships, you need to ask the LORD to sever the soul ties; but first, you need to repent for your sins in and outside of that relationship. As long as the soul tie exists, that person will continue to write upon your life. You can say to them to stay away from you; but your heart will still have traces of them in it, and your soul will still bear the residue of that relationship, sculpting all of your future relationships. Understand that GOD only called one character into your life to be with you intimately and that is your husband or your wife. Anyone else is an intruder.

THE VILLAIN

Every great story involves a villain. The villain is usually the "bad guy" or "bad girl" who is trying to destroy all mankind. In our lives, however, the villain is the person or people who have tried to destroy our lives, our reputations, and our families. In truth, the villain is Satan and people are just his pawns.

You won't find a person alive who doesn't have a few villains to tell you about. Whether those villains are 'active' villains; still trying to bring the person down, or if they are 'inactive' villains from times of old, they are always memorable.

Your story does involve villains; that's without question. But, people often look at the "bad guy" as a carrier of death, misery, and all things bad, when in truth, your villain has two hands. In one hand, the villain carries the evil that he or she wants to inflict upon you and in the other hand; the villain carries wisdom. Yes, the villain was likely sent by Satan, but in every attack is a lesson that yields a blessing. The trouble is, we often see the bad, and we want to fight that, but we ignore what we should be grabbing onto. You should NEVER undergo an attack without coming out of it wiser than you went into it. Every time life punches you; you'd better open its hands and pull out the goodies, and then you can punch it back with the WORD of GOD.

The average person looks for their villains, and they often predetermine who their villains are based on how they look, something they said, or something they did. In most cases, these people are not their villains, but they themselves become the villain of the people they have prejudiced. The concept of a villain has been changed due to the fact that people often see anyone that offends them or their way of thinking as their villains, when this is not the truth. Everyone you meet and everyone you know is at a certain point in their lives and in many cases, you are at a different place in your life. You may be wiser or not as wise as them and this often breeds contention because man has grown to believe that every person who does not agree with him is evil. This is evidence that the heart of man is increasingly wicked. The truth is that GOD called you to walk in a certain direction, and HE has called the people you come in contact with to walk in a certain direction. Along your path of obedience, you may meet up for a season, but your paths may fork off in different directions in HIM. Nevertheless, the average man believes that when the road forks off, and the time comes for him to go his own way that you should accompany him on his journey, but when you choose to follow your own GOD blazed trail; he may see you as his villain. The average man thinks that his GOD assigned place is wide enough to accommodate you because he does not understand that the road to CHRIST is narrow. He gave you intimate details about his life, and he thought you'd be there until the end of time, helping him with his assignments and his trials. To follow his path, of course, you'd have to become a villain of GOD because you were called to a certain place by HIM, to do a certain thing in a certain time, and if you're not found with HIM, you are found against HIM. This is why you will see so much contention amongst believers. People don't understand or want to understand that other souls are not their personal properties or accessories.

Oftentimes, the real villains are the people who we allow

within the closest proximity to our hearts. These are the people to whom we have given pens and pencils to write on our lives because we trust them enough to allow them in. Family can be your number-one villain because we were trained to believe that they have the right to mark our lives because we share the same blood type. The people who never grow outside of the "familiar" mentality rarely go far in life.

What is the distinction between the pens and pencils as mentioned? Well, a pencil has an eraser and what is written with a pencil can be erased. A great example of a pencil mark is an attempt to assassinate your character through gossip. In most cases, this can be erased because the people who GOD gave important roles in your lives won't believe gossip, therefore, it won't affect your story. It'll only be received by people who don't have important roles in your life, and it'll be forgotten the next time they get their helping of juicy gossip from the next gossiper.

A pen has no eraser. Whatever is written by the pen is permanent. A child from a sinful relationship is a great example. Of course, you don't want to erase the child, but you wish you could erase the sin itself. Another great example of a pen mark is a marriage to the wrong person. Many would argue that they could erase the marriage by divorcing their spouse, but this isn't true. Once you get married, you will remain married unless GOD releases you from that union. You can walk away, but in GOD'S eyes, you are still married. A less dramatic example of a pen mark would be the loss of a job, loss of a loved one, a stint in jail or prison, or anything that leaves a permanent mark on your life or your life's record. Even some gossip can be labeled as a pen mark because it causes irreparable damage to your life, relationships, or some area in your life. Gossip can only be in its most potent form when the person spreading it has some inside track to our lives and what they are spreading has some truth to it.

The closer a person is to you, the more they will know about you. Someone who does not have a close relationship with you can't really spread gossip so damaging that it makes a noticeable change to your life. Now, it's not impossible, but it's less likely to happen because they don't have an inside view of your life. They simply have a source or a hunch and this waters down their words, but the closer someone is to you, the more truth they know about you. That's why your greatest enemies are usually the people who are closest to you.

People can manage to keep the deepest and darkest secrets from your past until you dare to rise up and do something great with your future. If you want to really see who your villains are, dare to rise to greatness and watch the swords that are drawn. Some of the people who you wrote off as the villains in your stories will rise up and stand with you against those swords, and some of the people who you stood by will be the ones who stand up against you. The more you discover the character that you are, the more your eyes will open to see the characters around you. When you're blind to your destiny, you are blind to everything else. You can see with your natural eyes, but dare to go so far in GOD, serving HIM in obedience, seeking out wisdom, and interceding for others and watch how much your story changes. What looked like a horror story to you will turn out to be one of the greatest romance, action, inspirational stories that could ever be told. That's when you can truly say that someone needs to write a book about your life because you have been so far down that people have thrown your book away because they had already decided how they believed it was going to end. Then, all of a sudden, GOD shifted you in a way that only GOD can do, and when those same people looked back up at you, your story had taken on a different tune. And these same people won't be able to deal with you because they'd written you off. How dare you rise up and be blessed! These are your real villains. These are the characters who will rise up to try and assassinate your character. That man who took your girlfriend isn't a villain; he was sent to remove a character from your story that wasn't supposed to be there in the first place. You've got to grow to know who your villains really are and who they are not. The people who just promptly got on your nerves and went away aren't your villains; they are just people who came to clean off the stage so that the next scene in your life can play out without incident.

Villains are interesting characters because they cause repeated cycles of hurt in your life. They can only do this when they are in your life and shouldn't have been there in the first place. Review your life and think back to the person who has brought you heartache over the years. You kept them around, for some reason, or another. You probably pitied them or you have remembered all of the nice things they have done for you, ignoring the bad things they have done to you. A villain can be extremely nice and helpful, but that doesn't mean they are your friends, and it doesn't mean they love you. Often times, they are just patiently hating you and waiting on the right moment to do the wrong things.

In order to go further in life, you have to recognize who your villains are. Once you learn to recognize the role of certain people in your life, it will be easier to live a drama-free life. Every character in your story has a role assigned by GOD, but when you give them roles outside of what GOD intended them to have, you will cause another villain to rise up in your life. It's not their fault because you assigned them a role that they were not skilled to fill, so they defaulted back to their real character.

One of the prayers I have found to be essential to my growth is asking the LORD to remove the people from my life that HE did not call in it and to position the people in my life that HE did call in it into their rightful places. I understand that I place people in the wrong places according to how my emotions are stirring at that moment, only later to regret it. We have a place in our lives that we want them to fit in and this often opposes where they actually do fit in. You may meet a woman who sounds so much like you today. She has dealt with many of the issues you have dealt with, and she is where you are, but this doesn't necessarily mean that she is where you will be. So, you grow more and more, but she's comfortable where she is. Nevertheless, she doesn't want to lose you as a friend, and she does not like this growth thing you are experiencing because it is threatening the friendship. To stop it, she begins to attack you with words and speak word curses over your life when you are not around. Now, she has become your villain because she has direct access to you and as such, she has the right to speak into your life. You were supposed to guard your heart, but you let her in because she was just like you at that moment. Now she has drawn up a campaign of words and attempts to bring you back down to her size. Trying to disassociate yourself from her will prove to be a task because she was banking on the relationship working out. She has invested time, effort, and gifts into this union, and she is determined to collect on her interest. These are the people who have to be prayed and fasted out because we have developed soul ties through our associations with them. Yeah, you could beat them out, but that's not GOD'S way, and it definitely won't do anything to destroy the soul tie. They are simply characters that were given roles that they weren't mature or skilled enough to have.

People also like to create villains in their stories. Man feels pushed to succeed when a villain is on his heels. You will find a lot of people who view just about everyone as their villain. Don't speak to them at the supermarket, and you're suddenly their enemy, even though you honestly didn't see them. Correct them and you're their enemy. Some people need a villain to push them a fart's distance forward. These are characters who have taken their eyes off GOD, and they are focused on getting to a certain place in life; but because there is no wisdom found in them, they draw near to the wrong people. Having been burned a time or two, they begin to see everyone as a villain. These are the "Bonnie and Clyde" types who often pair up with people just like themselves and develop this "us against the world" mentality. If you bring them into your story, you will become a villain in their story, and they will have a dramatic role in yours. Be careful who you are handing pens and pencils to.

Remember these points:
1. A villain isn't someone who hurt you once; it's someone who has had access to hurt you again and again. Most villains don't make themselves known until you get to a certain height in CHRIST or to a certain level of success, and that's when they will draw their weapons. This is why GOD drives people away from you all of a sudden. You thought they were there for life, when GOD saw otherwise.
2. A person who burns you once or twice is simply a scene in your story. They don't have enough power to keep burning you, so they use the opportunities they do have to heat you up. This isn't a villain; it's a scene. You can determine how the story ends with them by choosing whether to serve the LORD in obedience or to serve the flesh and give them what you feel is their just reward. But remember, when you attack a short-term character, he or she becomes a long-time fixture in your book.
3. Be careful who you share your intimate details with. A villain will always want to know the most about you so that they can use it whenever they see an opportunity to reveal themselves without the masks.
4. A villain can and often does start off as a friend. Pray about everyone who enters your life.
5. A great man or woman will have even greater enemies. Do you really think that little Bubba living in a box could be considered a villain to a billionaire? Of course not. So, when

you find people you respect attacking you, it is only because they see greatness in you that exceeds the greatness they thought they had!

6. Every character in your story will assume a role, and it isn't always the role you want them to have.

7. Every character in your story comes in and writes on your life. If you don't like what they are writing, why are they a part of your story?

8. Just because they are related to you doesn't mean they have the right to access you. Some of the greatest villains you will ever have will be people who you are related to. Some even being the very people who grew up in the same household as you.

9. A potential villain is always looking for an opportunity to tell you how they feel about you and what they think you need to change. This includes people, who for no reason or explanation, suddenly stop talking to you or start to turn their nose up at you. These souls wait for an opportunity for you to ask them what is wrong so they can tell you what they don't like about you. If a person doesn't like a part of your personality (and it's not a trait that offends GOD), it could only mean that they were and are not supposed to be in your life or in the position they have in your life. When someone does not understand the height of something, they always try to chop it down. When someone feels that you are acting like you're 'better than them', it's not that you truly act this way; sometimes, it's the GOD in you that brings conviction to them every time you are around. Therefore, in order to please them, you have to 'come down'; off your 'high horse'. Interpretation: You need to 'dumb down' so they can relate to you. That person will become a villain with a pen if you let them write in your book. Let folks be mad at you because it's their right to do so. Adding to that, you don't have to ask people what you did to offend them if you know that you haven't done anything against them.

10. Know when a chapter ends and a new one begins. Anytime

you find strife in the midst, that means that chapter has ended and GOD is no longer in the midst. We are to gather together in HIS Name, but when the flesh starts to gather, the flesh starts to fight.

<u>WHOSE VILLAIN ARE YOU?</u>

Have you ever met someone who seems to find something wrong in just about everyone? They are always complaining about what this or that person did to them, and their life is a continuous circle of betrayal and hurt. If you stay around them too long, you will be the next person who has betrayed them. Maybe you said "no" to their demands, and they just don't know how to handle this word, or maybe you didn't do as they asked you to do. So, now, you have become the villain in their stories.

Every great story has a villain; we've already come to that conclusion, but oftentimes, people create villains to serve their own hurts. When someone is hurting on the inside because of past betrayals, they often deal with their hurt by hurting others. This goes hand in hand with the old adage, "Hurt people hurt people." People like to have a face to connect to their enemy, and when there are some unresolved issues lurking in them, they will look for the template of an enemy in you. Maybe you look like the man who stole his bicycle, or you look like the woman who took her boyfriend. Maybe you just sound like someone who hurt them, or you act like someone who betrayed them. People will find reasons to place someone's picture on your face and then box away at you.

Sometimes people can befriend you and stick around you for

years, having stored you up in their heart as their villain. They've kept you close because you are what motivates them to push harder for success. This is reality! People do bring others around them just for motivational purposes. A great example would be that girl from high school who was beautiful, conceited, and nowhere close to humble. The world loves to make fun of this character in the movies because you will find them in just about every school. She has friends whom the world refers to as "drones." These friends are often not as pretty as her as or popular as her, but they admire her, so they do everything she wants them to do. They beat up her enemies, buy her gifts, and simply make her look good. But, in her heart, she often does not see them as friends; they are her villains, and she will talk about each character in her circle to another character in her circle. These girls motivate her, and this is why she keeps them close.

You need to know what role you are playing in the lives of others. You just may find that you are the villain in their story, and every story that involves a villain, involves a victory over that villain. People can stick around you and look for ways to defeat what they see you as, their Goliath. I find this especially true amongst women. It goes without saying that most women do not like to have a lot of women as friends because women often look for villains, or they'll transfer you to the villain section in their stories in a heartbeat. I've literally had a couple of former female friends get angry with me because I didn't answer the phone when they called. They took it personally because with some women, they believe if they are having a problem, and you don't answer the phone; you have just shown yourself as a villain. Men do this as well, but not so easily.

Then there are some families who have this one character who can never do right by the family. He or she is always in trouble because they did something outside of the family's familiar limitations. Are you that family member? If so, it's probably because you are being called to come outside of the familiar and embrace a life that is not surrounded by family. You often have to let go of family to move into destiny.

Whose villain are you? If you find you are the villain in someone's story or slowly becoming a villain in their story, remove yourself from their story! Don't wait for them to get the chance to bring down their giant of you! If you can never seem to do right by someone, no matter how hard you try, you are their villain. The sad thing is, people create villains in their hearts so that they can feel motivated to move forward. These same people don't look for one-time or part-time villains. You have to understand; the villain is often in the story until the very end of the story. The story ends when the villain has been overcome or killed, and their peace is restored.

Look at some families where a person has been murdered, for example. It's quite understandable that they are hurting, and they want to hold someone accountable for their loss. In comes a murder suspect and the police don't have enough evidence to rightfully prove that this person is the actual murderer, but they arrest him or her anyway and charge them with the murder. During court proceedings, the family learns there is absolutely no evidence that the accused is the murderer, but there is plenty of evidence to suggest otherwise. I've seen this on some of those television shows; where a person has spent decades in prison, only to be vindicated later. Anyhow, the family focuses all of their hurts, anger and fury on the person who has been made to play the face of the killer because they need somewhere to channel this hurt and rage.

Hurt people are the same way. They need somebody somewhere to stand in as a face for them to channel their rage and hurt. When you came in and auditioned to be a part of their story, you obviously forgot to find out what role you were auditioning for. It's easy to find out who people want you to be by simply talking to them and praying about them. I've had a few cases where a woman or two tried hard to become a part of my story, and this always sends up red flags. When a person is adamant about getting into your life, often times, something is wrong. Anyhow, after talking with them a few times, I discovered that I "looked like" some woman who hurt them in some kind of way. Most women have had this to happen to them. Another woman comes along and just goes all out of her way to get into your story and a few phone calls later, she reveals that you look just like the woman who stole her husband. Now, in this, she just told you what role she wants you to serve. You are the template for this other woman, and she wants to vent about how she felt when 'you' did what 'you' did and what she'd like to do with 'you'. She may say this woman's name, but you are now her template, her villain and the giant she has to overcome. She has what I call "video game" mentality. She believes that once she overcomes you, she can move to the next level, when in truth, she needs to overcome her unforgiveness. That's her giant, but you have a face; unforgiveness does not, so you'll have to do for now.

When friends and family gossip about you, you are their villain. You can't go around trying to alter how someone sees you. Too many times, people try to open their loved one's eyes hoping they (the loved ones) could see them for who they really are. Have you ever tried to put eyeglasses on a dog? What does he do with them? He looks up and immediately decides he doesn't like the view, and he removes the glasses without hesitation. This is how people do. Sometimes, they don't want the truth; they want a villain to complete their stories.

Know your roles and don't sign up for any that are scheduled to have bad endings. You have to be willing to walk away from dead relationships in order to live. The best way to minister to the people you love is not through your words, but through your life. If you walk away and stay in CHRIST, HE will bless you. One day, when they come in contact with you again, they will witness the change that GOD has made in you. This is your opportunity to tell them about CHRIST JESUS and possibly have them listen a little bit more than they would have listened before your transition.

Remember this: If the only role open in someone's story is that of the villain, don't audition for it. In addition, don't believe what people say; believe what they do. It's your choice who you want to be for others, but if you find that you are the villain; it's time for you to exit that story.

OTHER CHARACTER ROLES

Every great story has the person or people who need to be rescued from the villain. In the end, the hero comes running out to save the victim or victims and peace is restored. In romance stories, the good girl is set up with the good strong guy, and they ride off into the sunset together, leaving the viewers to wonder whatever became of their lives. In life, we still have these characters living among us. There are the victims who look for rescuers and there are the hero types that look for someone who needs rescuing. Knowing the role your character is playing will help you identify where a change is needed.

At one point in my life, I was broken to pieces. I was victimized over and over again, and I now know that at that time, I was looking for a hero. I wanted someone to save me from the villains who'd molested me or the villains who'd oppressed me. I loved movies where the good girl would eventually be rescued, and all of her enemies were slain. That's because my heart was wicked, and my ways were perverted. I didn't realize at that time that I had already been rescued. I simply needed to rescue myself from the evil that resided in me, and I could only do this by turning to the ONE that had rescued me, CHRIST JESUS. As we grow in HIS perfect knowledge and learn our identities, we begin to shed that victim mentality and walk as more than a conqueror through CHRIST JESUS.

Victim mentality can be seen in the way one walks, heard in the way one talks, and displayed in their personalities. When one plays the victim, they are always looking for a hero to round the corner. Instead, all of these horrible characters keep coming in and pretending to be heroes, only to victimize the broken even more. They are no worse than the victim because the victim is trying to assign a role that only GOD can fill to a mere man or woman, and this is too great of a role for anyone to take on. No one can rescue you from misery, but GOD. No one can heal or restore you, but GOD. No amount of apologies will make those wounds disappear; the only words that will clean them up and heal them is the WORD of GOD, and until the victim understands this, they'll continually be victimized.

I even thought of the people who I'd done while a youth. For a long time, I forgave others, but I didn't know how to forgive myself because I had hurt people. If I misguided someone, I would come back and try to re-guide the, hoping this time to be a better mentor, but I found that I was still trying to fill the role of GOD. Our job is to repent and move forward, making sure those who are broken know that we are changed creatures, and that GOD can change them too. When you stand in trying to rescue someone who does not want to be rescued, they will assign roles to you that were reserved for GOD, and you'll go crazy trying to fulfill the duties of these roles. You have to stop erecting yourself as that villain of old and see yourself as GOD sees you, whole and renewed. And never play into someone's brokenness because in their state of thinking, they will break you. Don't be a victim of self-pity.

People with the victim mentality tend to always see others as villains because their sight is perverted. These are your characters who take offense very easily, and these are the characters we initially learned to be gentle with. If you sent them a text message, you'd put a little smiley face in it to keep them from thinking you were trying to be offensive. If you had missed their phone call, you'd call them back, apologizing and explaining why you didn't take the call. If you advised them, you would follow up each piece of advice with an "if you want to" or a "but you may be different," because they are victims and victims act offensively. I had to learn to stop treading softly with these characters because in trying not to offend them, you are actually submitting to their demons. The truth is a sword and it does cut. Cut that devil out of them with the truth. In most cases, we don't even realize how we handle people until we consciously look at ourselves. What is on someone's life is often evident by how you handle them and how you perceive others is often evidence of what is on your life. Here are a few examples:

Example 1: Desiree knows the WORD of GOD. As a matter of fact, she is a pastor; yet she is an active fornicator. She calls Wendy to tell her about the series of trials and tribulations that has been following her, including this ailment that she has recently been diagnosed with. She asks Wendy to pray for her, but Wendy first has to understand that she is either going to be a participant in Desiree's sin by turning her head and praying for Wendy, or she's going to come against the sin and tell Desiree the truth. Desiree may see it as the devil attacking her, but it is more than likely a chastening, or better put, a spiritual butt-whooping. Have you ever tried to stand in the way when your natural daddy was whooping one of your siblings? What happened if you did? You got their licks! So, Wendy begins to minister to Desiree and tell her that her fornication has risen up before the LORD, and because she is a pastor, she is not only affecting herself, but she is imparting what is on her to the congregation. So, Wendy lovingly and authoritatively rebukes her friend, but Desiree doesn't want to hear it. "If you're going to pray for me, pray for me, but if not, don't pray for me! I already know everything that you're preaching! You forget; I'm a pastor! So, please forgive me if I'm not moved by your speech!" Now, do you see the rebellion against GOD in her? And here, many characters would have prayed that the whooping stop and tried to stand between Desiree and the LORD'S rod and got the beat down of their lives. Desiree, in her own mind, was a victim of a devil attacking her, but she refused to understand that the WORD of GOD is truth, even for her. She wanted to be prayed for, but she did not want the truth.

This is how the truth works; HE comes on the inside and heals us from within. So many leaders today would have said to Desiree, "This too shall pass! The devil will get his hands off of you! I am rebuking that devil on your behalf! No weapon formed against you shall prosper!" Not knowing that the weapon wasn't formed against her, the Sword of the WORD simply cut her with the truth! If Desiree wants to be a victim, that's her right; but you should never play into that role unless you want to be her story's villain. If you badger her and try to force her to see that she's wrong, you are operating in pride. GOD never forces us to make peace with the truth; HE gives us the right to accept it or reject it. She chose to reject it, so your next move is to pray that GOD continues to deal with her heart. As for that diagnosis, you need to understand that fornication is not only a sin against GOD, but it is a sin against our own bodies. That is, we are allowing death to come into our bodies anytime we engage in fornication since the wages of sin is death. This is the cause or root of many of the ailments that attack believers today because they let it in. Should you stand by and watch her die? No, but the only thing you can do is tell her the truth and hope that she'll repent and sin no more. She chose to be a victim. That's her choice!

Example 2: William calls his new co-worker Brandon to see if he could catch a ride to work with him on Monday. It was Friday and William's car had said its final good-byes, so he knew that he would need a ride on Monday. William is not the type of person who likes to wait until the last minute, so he calls Brandon on Friday to see if he'd be able to pick him up. Brandon, however, is a victim. He has been victimized so much in his life, and he is constantly reliving each episode because he hasn't forgiven anyone of his assailants. So, William's call seemed suspicious to Brandon. Why would he call on Friday? Why didn't he wait until Sunday? William lives less than a mile away from Brandon, so this is the reason he called Brandon for a ride. He would have to pass his house heading to work anyway, so why not call? Brandon's wife is very much into being fitted, and she likes to jog two miles a day in the direction of William's home. Now, Brandon has concocted this evil plot in his mind; believing that William and his wife may be having an affair. So, he begins to be more attentive towards his wife and display rude behaviors towards his co-worker. The more Brandon investigates, the more he believes that he's on to their scheme.

Let's just end it there. Brandon's perception was his deception. A series of innocent events activated what was already in him. Victims are often already victims when they begin to accuse others of intentionally harming them or betraying them. Our perception causes us to betray ourselves into putting situations together and making them fit. In this, we feel smart and untouchable, so we continue adding things together that don't go together. Brandon's perception is evidence of something going on inside of him that has robbed him of his peace and caused him to look for villains. Sadly enough, Brandon's wife has to play the role of the villain when his insecurities begin to flare up.

Another character is the hero character. Heroes are usually victims trying to vicariously rescue themselves by rescuing others. They love the idea and the feeling of playing someone's savior. Now, there are some legitimate heroes out there who don't walk around wearing an invisible cape, but there is also a common hero impersonator who preys on others for his or her own personal gain. For example, that man or that woman who wants to rescue someone's spouse from what they perceive to be a bad marriage. Now, their motive isn't necessarily to rescue the spouse, but to feed some type of void within themselves and once this thirst is quenched; they usually go about looking for more endangered spouses. Then there are the characters who I like to refer to as demolition heroes. They like to tear you down and make you believe that something is wrong with you. If you receive their diagnosis, they will proceed to try and rescue you and build you up how they want you to be. Some parents even do this to their very own children because they like the taste of being a hero, even though they are twisted demolition workers who knock down perfectly good buildings to erect buildings that have to stand on their words to stay erect. Another hero is the one who rescues someone from a bad situation only to lead them to a worse situation. An example would be the aspiring pastor who visits a church and tries to find a head position in that ministry. He or she then proceeds to try and convince the congregation, member by member, that their church is evil, and that they should follow his or her ministry. These people, often times, did not need rescuing, but if they follow this character; they will need rescuing.

The hero character is an interesting character because they will often put themselves in harm's way to fulfill a need therein. In our stories, we need our villains, but we can't play the victim, and we can't play the hero. CHRIST has the role of the hero, and HE gave us the role of "more than a conqueror through CHRIST JESUS." When someone comes in trying to save you from a situation or a person; beware. For example, there are some broken women who have been hurt tremendously by the men in their lives, and our hearts do go out to them, but they continued to live in their unforgiveness and developed a hate for men in general. These women are very dangerous because they are always looking for evidence to support their belief that all men are monsters. When one of these characters befriends a woman who is, for example, in an abusive relationship, they (the heroes) usually volunteer to "take care of the problem."

Why? Because this is giving them the opportunity to attack every man who has ever harmed them. This abusive man, to them, is the devil, and they want to enjoy watching him blink for the last time. He is simply a template of the men in which these women have been victims of.

Some people come along and rescue you only to put you in a smaller prison. A good example of this would be a friend who doesn't like your other friend...so they battle it out over that "piece of property." (Hey, sometimes demons battle over territory, but people don't want to understand that.) She comes in and basically tells you she does not like your friend and feels that she is not really a good friend to you. To prove it, she decides to go undercover and talk about you to this friend. Now, this doesn't happen in adult relationships very often, but amongst preteens and young adults, it is fairly common. Anyhow, whatever was said about you is carried back to you from the investigative buddy. After she has successfully broken up the friendship, she'll proceed to take the former friend's place. Problem is, she's often worse than the former friend. She simply wanted to remove everyone from around you who she felt would be a threat to her intentions with you.

What if you are one of these characters? You can change by repenting and feeding on the WORD of GOD daily. Ask the LORD to deliver you from this mindset. One of the heroes that I found myself trying to be was to rescue women who were like how I used to be. I could relate to them, so I would set out to tell them about my past; show them what GOD has done for me and offer to help them to get to their blessed places. The LORD had to deal with me about my manner of rescue because I didn't understand that you can't rescue someone who doesn't want to be rescued. And you can never rescue people with things and talks of going to great heights in their careers. Deliverance is a step-by-step process, and just like I had to start with the first step, so do they. I was feeding their idea of being able to skip a few steps and jump straight to the top, and this was causing them to want to seek GOD for the wrong reasons. They wanted the financial independence and the perks of being HIS children, but they rarely talked about simply doing it for the love of GOD.

Again, many hero impersonators come along and place people in bondage. They rescue them from one situation and bind them in another one. Think about how a loan company works. I saw a commercial where a loan company was offering high-interest loans to people who wanted to pay off other loans. That's like having your potential kidnapper pay your current kidnapper his required ransom so that the new kidnapper can ransom you for even more. He's a criminal with a business plan.

There are many types of hero impersonators out there, but GOD will ring an alarm in our hearts anytime these people are trying to rescue us from another person or situation. Now, there are some cases where someone may truly know something that you don't, and they'll proceed to warn you, but impersonators like to take it further. Impersonators almost always try to take the place of the person whom they helped move out.

Who is your hero character? Who is rescuing you from what? GOD will never share HIS glory with you or anyone else; therefore, we have to know and recognize that even when we see the face of a man, GOD does use people to come into our stories and offer us a way of escape. A way of escape does not imply that you will be carried out of captivity, but it does imply that the door is open for you to walk free. When someone comes in and erects themselves as our rescuers, we need to be conscious about their motives and prayerful. A righteous man or woman will always give the glory to GOD, but a person with selfish motives will always hang a yoke around your neck and remind you of what they've done for you. A hero impersonator will always make the people who they claim to have rescued feel indebted to them. They may not speak directly and say that one is indebted to them, but they will say things like, "Why can't you come? I was hoping you could come because I spent a lot of money buying your favorite food, and you know when I punched that guy out that was messing with you; I sprained my leg, so it wasn't easy standing over that hot stove. But, I did it for you....nevertheless, if you can't come; I guess I just have to understand." This is manipulation, and it means you are dealing with a manipulative character. Get him or her out of your story and fast! ***"Owe no man anything, but to love one another: for he that loveth another hath fulfilled the law" (Romans 13:8).*** If this character loaned you money, give it back as fast as you can. If this character rescued you from another person, thank them and be on your way. If this character took you in and fed you, tally up what you think you owe them and be on your way. Now, if they told you that you could stay there for free and eat freely, then you owe them nothing; be on your way.

GOD may use you to bring people out of their Egypts, but never ever take credit for it. You are not the hero; GOD is. You were and are simply a vessel and to think about it any other way is evil. If you feel indebted to someone, pray it off. This is just a yoke that Satan has placed on your mind. Be free of it. The best gift you can give someone is to share the WORD. Remember, CHRIST paid the ultimate price and anything you do or someone else does doesn't even come close to what HE did.

CHARACTER ASSASSINATION

We know assassination to be the killing of an individual of a certain rank or power. If a store clerk was killed, it would be referred to as murder; but if the mayor, governor, president or any individual with a certain degree of celebrity was killed; it would be referred to as assassination. Character assassination usually refers to the attack against a person's character or name. When someone tries to assassinate your character, what they are doing is simply trying to get people to see you as they see you or see you as the character that they are portraying you to be. It is their attempt to kill your name.

Now, if you're human, you've probably talked badly about someone before. They made you mad or hurt your feelings, and you used the first set of ears that you could find to release your fury into. After it was over, you felt relieved that you'd released what was pent up inside of you, but now you had another problem. Would the person you just got through speaking with go back and share your rant with the person you were talking about? Of course, as we mature in CHRIST, we have to put idle speech behind us and learn to communicate directly with one another. When we don't, we too are participating in character assassination.

A lot of people spend too much of their day, week and life fuming over something someone has said about them. Minutes tick by and then hours; before they know it, they've spent an entire day on the phone talking about the person who is attempting or has attempted to assassinate their character. There are a few things that you should know that will surely help you get over what people say and think about you and move on to the next chapter of your life.

First, you are the starring character in your story, and GOD is your illustrator, editor and so on. No one can assassinate who you are without your permission. If someone doesn't know who you are, they can't really go about assassinating your name, even if they know your name and have seen you around. People can try to tarnish your good name when they don't know you, but it usually fizzles out quickly because they are not presenting enough facts about you and your life to capture the attention of others. The only people who will listen to them are people who don't like you anyway. However, when someone is close to you and knows your personal life, failures, hang-ups and struggles; they can easily attempt to assassinate your character because they can present facts about you. This is especially true for immediate family members because they often know how big of a sinner you once were. Therefore, anyone who spews venom on your name needs to be close enough to bite you before that venom takes effect. If someone is close to you, and they bite you, you have yourself to blame; especially when you have grown older and have gotten to know the LORD. Maya Angelou's quote says it best, "If someone tells you who they are; believe them." Better yet, if someone shows you who they are, you'd better believe them. If they've burned you once, why do you think that they won't burn you twice? Unless a person is changed by GOD, they will remain the same, and they will continue to do the things that they are accustomed to doing.

Families often tolerate betrayal from one another because many are taught that this is the norm, and they have to stick together in this cruel world. Yet, many will endure some of the cruelest acts from one another against themselves and their children just to stay a part of the close-knit family. Again, it is those individuals who are closest to you that will have the range to make life-altering assassination attempts against your character. If you were the governor of your state, and someone on your staff tried to assassinate you but failed, would you let them come back to work for you? No. You'd have them arrested, and you'd terminate their employment. You'd probably even get a restraining order against them should they get out of jail.

Why is it that when certain people attempt to assassinate your character, you allow them near you again to make a second and third attempt? Is it because you believe that forgiving them is dealing with them? You can forgive someone and love them from a distance. JESUS let Judas near HIM because JESUS had an assignment here on earth, and Judas was a part of HIS story. HE knew who Judas was, and HE even let Judas carry the money bag, even though Judas was a thief. Again, this was because Judas was a part of HIS story, and CHRIST'S story was already written before HE came into the flesh. What HE did was fulfill what is written. You don't have to tolerate your Judas unless GOD says otherwise. If your Judas is not a part of GOD'S story for you, then you're in sin trying to deal with him or her because evil communication ruins useful habits.

Secondly, remember when someone assassinates a person it is always someone of great rank. No one will attempt to assassinate your character unless you have great rank in their eyes or the eyes of others. When you're down in sin, you don't rank high enough for someone to want to kill your name because your sin is doing that for them. As you begin to rank on a different scale, you become target for more and more attempts to destroy your name. I was watching some well-known preachers on YouTube one day, and I noticed that whenever I would type in their name, the search results would display a video that claims to be exposing them. I typed in "Juanita Bynum," and a video claiming to expose her came up. Of course, I didn't open it because I don't lend my ears to such foolishness. Another time, I did a search for "Joyce Meyers," and there it was again, another video claiming to expose her. If any man has a rank of celebrity status, you will begin to see videos and articles come up that are attempts to assassinate their character. This is because they rank highly in the eyes of the one who posted the video, and the poster has decided to attempt to bring them down with hopes of destroying their character.

I can remember laughing when I did a Google search for a character that I know and his name came up with a lot of negative feedback. He had a lot of good feedback, but people were creating whole blog pages dedicated to assassinating his name. It was funny to me, and I decided to make a mental note to tell his wife that he's moving on up. Until you have had someone to try and assassinate your character; you haven't arrived yet. Character assassination attempts are the first sign that you are positioned in a place that folks feel they can't reach you, and they need to bring you down because they see you as being up. I told my friends that if I ever see a negative page dedicated to me, I'm going to save it, print it and frame it. That's a trophy!

Next, a name can only be successfully assassinated if you're guilty, or you're pretending to be who you are not. If you went to the supermarket with Cousin Shannon, and you stole a pack of peanuts, then you're guilty. If Cousin Shannon decides to advertise it to the world, he isn't assassinating your character, he is exposing your real character. However, if Cousin Shannon accused you of stealing a pack of peanuts, and you hadn't stolen a pack of peanuts, then Shannon is guilty of attempting to assassinate your character. It's up to you if you give him a second chance. You fire the first bullet at your character; however, when you pretend to be who you are not.

Let's create another character and call her Brandy. Brandy sees a group of girls that are a little rough around the edges, and Brandy admires them. She wants so badly to hang out with them because they seem fearless, and they're always laughing; but Brandy's a good girl. She's had maybe three fights in her whole life, and they've been with her little brother. She makes good grades in school; she's respectful, loving and responsible; nevertheless, she views these girls as free and mysterious. She's been bound up behind that "good girl" mask for a while, and she wants to try her hands at being bad. She starts trying to hang around these women; cursing continuously hoping to impress them. They sense that she is nothing like them, so they decide to set her up for a fight. There is a rival group of girls living a few yards away from the gang's hangout, so they ask Brandy to go down there and beat up the girl wearing all black. They say that Brandy needs to prove herself to them, and they say that this girl is weak; she's been taken down by several of them. They're lying. This girl has the strength of twelve men and a bear, and she's beaten everyone who has ever attempted to approach her. The gang, however, has been wise enough to avoid her. Brandy hurries on down the street and from a distance, they can see Brandy start the argument and then pass the first punch. One of the girls takes out her cell phone to record the fight. Brandy's on the ground, pleading for her life, but no one comes to her rescue. Everyone is laughing at her, even the people she'd attempted to impress.

That type of story is very common. When you don't like the fit of your own skin, you'll find out how hard it is to try to fit in the skin of someone else. If these girls went about telling everyone that Brandy is a phony, and that she got beat up by the giant girl on 5th street, they aren't assassinating her character; they are presenting the character that they met. So, her good name may be tarnished because of a bad decision.

Lastly, your character can only die to the people who you know or the people who know you. In every family, there is a character that is talked about negatively all the time. It is usually the character that has a mental illness or the person who dares to go outside of the family's understanding. Let's create another character and call her Betty. Betty has worked hard to become the woman whom she is today, but her family only remembers Betty by the character that she was yesterday. Betty has overcome the generational curses that are on her family through CHRIST JESUS; therefore, she is always on the family's radar because she is different. Many may perceive her as being puffed up, but in truth; she's just changed. Betty goes to a family picnic and is disgusted by the behavior of her nieces and nephews, so she goes about, rebuking them and telling them what their behaviors would lead to. One of Betty's sisters notices her and decides to set her straight because Betty just corrected her child. She has already determined in her heart that Betty is too high-minded; therefore, Betty has no right to correct her children. The other sisters who are like her can correct them, but Betty cannot. She goes over to Betty and begins to scream at her, and this altercation leads to several people in the family standing around Betty and yelling at her. At this point, Betty decides that it is way past time to stop dealing with her family and to start new associations. Betty moves to a house a few cities away and to the people who are just meeting Betty, she is a great character. Her story has just started with them but to her family, Betty is everything awful, and they have already put out a hit on her character in their hearts.

If you're not a well-known figure, you don't have to worry about character assassination on a major scale; but you may deal with it at work, in relationships, at church and so on. It is still hurtful, and no one likes to see their name in the shredder, but if you knew that character assassination is the first sign that you have arrived in greatness; would it make a difference? Did you know that if you are called to do something great, on a large scale; you need to be prepared for character assassination attempts? If you can't deal with a Facebook status, for example, that someone posted up about you, you're not ready for greatness. If someone does something against you, and it's on your mind all day, you're not ready for elevation.

Pick out any well-known leader, Google their name and type the word "exposed" behind it. Watch all of those results. The more height a person has in the sights of man, the more his or her name will be subject to attempted assassinations. There are so many people who have greatness in them, but they are still in Pre-K when it comes to dealing with naysayers. Someone says something bad about them, and they spend the entire day on the phone trying to talk about the situation, get the gossiper told off and to just release the situation from their minds. They couldn't handle elevation just yet because when those posts came up about them, they'd sow too much time into reading them, responding to them and recovering from what was said.

One of the things we have to pray against is being troubled by what people say or think about us. That was a prayer that I had to pray. Once the LORD delivered me, I started losing friends. Why is that? It was because I started telling the truth and stopped being afraid of what they'd say in return. I started telling folks to stop fornicating, stop lying, and stop complaining. Just stop it! I said it in love, of course, but people don't want the truth in any form. They want someone to listen to them. Once you're delivered, you begin to love people more and this is what causes you to be truthful, and it helps you to appreciate those characters are truthful with you.

Stop worrying about what someone is saying about you. If you didn't rank in their eyes, they would keep quiet, but because you are great to them, they can't shut up about you. Does that make it feel better? It should. It made me feel better when I learned it. Let people talk; that's what they have a mouth for. When they speak ill of your name, this usually means that you should not have them within the range that you've had them in. They need to be further away from you so that they can't reach you to insert their venom. Whoever believes their report is just like them, so why would it matter that they believe it? Truth be told, the only time we are bothered by character assassination is when the character that is attempting to assassinate our names is one that we'd ranked in our hearts. Instead of pondering on it, let it be your "oops" moment of revelation, and you go away and learn from it.

CHARACTER AUDITIONS

One thing that always stands true in our stories is that people come along and audition to be a part of our stories. It could be that girl with whom you work who you've had plenty of conversations with, or it could be that man who stood in line behind you at the store. It doesn't matter where the characters come from, but what does matter is how they define you. They have a perception about you and at that moment in time, they feel like you'd make a great best-buddy for a particular place in their lives. We have to be extremely careful about bringing people in because we don't always know what role we are assuming in their hearts. Many people come in under the veil of assumption and find themselves disappointed when truth throws assumption out the window, and they get to see you for who you really are. Some people think that you have the key to their happiness, and others think that you will make great company in their misery. Whatever is in their hearts for you, it has to be discerned or uncovered through prayer because it is dangerous to just let any and everyone into your life just because they are nice.

Always pay attention to the words people are saying, and always listen to what GOD is speaking to you from within because when someone is auditioning to be a part of your story, they're coming in with some kind of expectation. Often times, when we cannot meet this expectation, we are shunned.

Take, for example, how I used to handle the characters who wanted me to be a part of their stories. I am a graphic designer; I publish books, help Christian businesses to start up and so on; therefore, many of the people who I met were through my businesses or ministry. One of the most common stories that headlined in my life was me letting people call me often and tell me all about their hardships. As a minister, I took this time to encourage them and try to help them to discover their talents. I pushed them towards business start-up because this is what I do, I help start businesses. I would help them to locate their talents and tell them how to get started. I'm overly thrilled when someone actually does take that talent and try to do something with it...so much so, that I used to offer them a free design to start them off or a discounted service. Anyhow, I'd get a call from them later on whining about another hardship that they're facing, and it always involved the lack of funds and a need for a service. So, again, I'd tell them about their talents and try to push them to dig up their talents and get to work, but it's like trying to crank up a car with no engine. They'd then ask for a free service, money, or something to help get them started, but in truth...they had no intention of launching. They wanted me to launch them, finance their dreams, and just give them everything for free. At this, I had to start saying "no" and sending out full-priced invoices for my services. That's when I'd find my phone number blocked, ugly emails, deletions from Facebook and so on. But, was it their fault? Yes and no. Yes, because they chose to let that mentality bind them and no, because I didn't pay attention to the role, they'd assigned me to in their lives. I guess one can say that I deceived them into believing I was easy to use. I played into this mentality by letting them have a drink of water in their deserts and then, by shutting it off and asking to be paid. My husband would always say to me, "Keep your friends separate from your business. Be friendly, but when they want to talk business, talk business and don't give discounts. That's how you shut all that down." Eventually, I listened and I watched my circle grow smaller because again, I did not pay attention to the role they'd assigned me to, and when I did catch on, I always ended the friendship by sending them an invoice when they requested another service. This invoice, to them, was like a "Dear John" letter.

Every character who wants to be a part of your story has a role they want to assume, and if we don't give them this role, they become dangerous, or they become absent. As we grow older in CHRIST and are elevated in CHRIST, the old characters in our lives have to re-audition for new parts in our lives. For example, think about when you were younger (for the ladies) and your friend had a baby. The two of you had been friends for years, but now she is a new mother, and you feel awkward and out of place. Now, you have to re-audition for her life because she isn't just your friend anymore, but she is now a mother. Sure, she lets you come over like you've been doing, but something about her changes. There are no more dances on the sofa or loud laughing throughout the house. Everything has to change, and at this moment, many women will look at their friends and review their friendships because now you are auditioning to be a part of their child's life. If you are a dangerous character, it is quite understandable that they don't want you in their lives anymore.

Pay attention to what people are saying. Most of the time, they are telling you how they view you and what they expect of you, but it is often hidden behind a compliment; nevertheless, we get so flattered that we let the truth tip-toe on by. I have literally had a few people tell me from the start that they wanted to have everything that I have. Now, by the time I ran into these types of people, I had already matured in CHRIST and knew EXACTLY what that meant, and I knew that they'd be dangerous to be around. Nobody can be you without first having been you. That means no one can step into your today without having endured the pangs of your yesterday; and I knew to let them in would mean I'd have to pray them out. Some people will audition to call you everyday, several times a day because they are not busy. Keep telling them that you'll call them back, and they'll bad-mouth you. Why is that? Because they thought that you'd play the part of the toilet. They wanted to flush their activities of the day in your ears and hang up when they felt better; however, it is your fault if you assume this role. When you try to change, often times, you invite contention since you are now living a life that they didn't audition to be a part of.

Again, people often tell us what they want; if not from the first conversation, they'll do it from the second or third. That's why you have to close all friendship auditions and ask the LORD to remove the wrong ones and position the right ones. Everybody has a price and often; it is a pretty hefty one. You just have to learn to read their invoices and decide if you want to pay that price.

Let's set up two scenarios to see if you can discern or determine the roles these two characters are auditioning for: Mark meets Malcolm at school, and they hit it off well. Mark is an all-around athlete, and he's pretty laid back. He has quite a few friends, but he's not into after-school hangouts. Malcolm, on the other hand, isn't so popular. He's pretty smart and just focuses his time at school on completing his work and going home. Mark tries to forge a friendship with Malcolm, and it finally pays off. He tells Malcolm about his declining grades and how they are threatening to kick him off the football team if he doesn't bring up his grade-point average. Being kindhearted and compassionate, Malcolm offers to help Mark with his studying, but Mark never seems to have much time to study. Instead, he asks Malcolm to do his homework for him. Of course, this is a very obvious case of Mark trying to use Malcolm. Mark had a role that was open, and he wanted Malcolm to assume this role.

Casey meets Samantha, and the two of them hit it off pretty well. They have so much in common! They are both chefs, and they are both inspired to start their own restaurants. Casey's special dish is her lobster chowder. The restaurant that she works at has seen an increase in business since she came there. Samantha's specialty is her shrimp a la diabla, and the restaurant that she works at now gets more orders for Sam's mean ole shrimp than any other menu specialty. Samantha and Casey are the best of friends, and they decide to do once a week cook-overs. Each Saturday one of the women cooks, and the other woman comes over and enjoys her friend's dish. One Saturday Casey calls and says that she has been craving Samantha's shrimp a la diabla. She asks her friend to cook it and she offers to bring the food, since her request is last-minute. She asks Samantha to text her the ingredients so that she can pick them up, and she does. After she arrives, she stands by Samantha telling her about this really cute guy that she'd met at the grocery store. What Samantha doesn't realize is that Casey simply wants to know how to cook everything that Samantha cooks, especially that shrimp a la diabla. After getting the recipes from Samantha, Casey retreats back to her life. She has no more interest in Samantha; matter of fact, Samantha is starting to come off as a nuisance. Why is this? Because Casey only wanted what Samantha had, and after she got it, she found no more use for Samantha.

There is no man who wants to get close to you just to be close. Any and everyone has a motive. Some motives are good while others are bad and most people who have bad motives don't realize that their intentions are evil. They simply see someone who fascinates them, and they pursue that person. If they win that person over, they begin to pursue what it is that fascinates them about that person; and if they come to the peak of it, they lose interest. This is human nature. Think about how people try to get close to a millionaire. They believe this character will help them to become millionaires or will help them out a little. Millionaires will not be friends with just anyone because they understand that people are not attracted to them; people are attracted to their wealth. People are, in reality, trying to get close to their money, and this is why people say that millionaires are "high-minded" or "prideful." It's not always true. Millionaires have to be very careful because they have something that people have been known to kill for, therefore, they have to stay around other millionaires, not because they think, they're better, but because they know better and the ones that don't, often pay for their ignorance with their lives.

What do the characters in your story see in you? I've met people who are aggressive and protective of the people in their circles. These characters usually have many people in their stories, but in reality, these people see them like "problem-solvers." Whenever a problem arises with another human being, they will call this character so that he or she will get involved and "solve" the problem. You will ALWAYS know who you are to a person when a problem arises in their lives because they have a character for every situation that they call when that situation arises. If you're their "pit-bull," they'll call you when they have someone they want you to attack. They won't always ask you directly to attack that person, but they will call you every time a problem arises. After putting on an emotional display about their problem, they wait to see how you will respond. If your response doesn't match the character that they thought you were; they will begin to disassociate themselves from you because their "pit-bull" has lost his bite. If they see you as an ATM, they'll call you every time they have money problems. They may not directly ask you for money, but they will hint around it, and many times; they'll actually call back and ask you upfront if you didn't catch the hint the first time. If people see you as a tutor, they'll call you when they need tutoring. The point is, whatever you are to a person will become obvious as you go along with them, and it'll always surface when they need you to act in the role they've retained you for.

So, the next time someone starts to spend a whole lot of time hanging around you, try to find out what it is about you that is attractive to them. A lot of times people are bound by their associations because they are expected to perform a certain role with this association. Anytime they act outside of how someone perceived them; they are ousted and ridiculed. So, they try to stay within the confines of someone's expectation of them; not understanding that they have been imprisoned and have denied themselves the blessings of GOD.

When characters come in, they define one another. "This girl is my best friend, and she'll beat up anyone who messes with me. That girl is an inspiration to me because she's doing everything I want to do. That girl is okay, but I like to hang around her because she can really cook, and her brother is super cute. The other girl is a great counselor; I call her every time I have a problem, and she helps me through it." Can you see how we see one another? You are defined by everyone around you, but if their definition of you does not match GOD'S definition, you'd better review your role. Sometimes their definition of you is good, and it is not limited to what they know about you. Nevertheless, often times, people limit others to roles and when those roles are breached, offense comes in and contention is unavoidable.

Always pray about the characters in your story and the characters who want to be a part of your story. Even a crazy man smiles and acts normal when he meets a woman, he's interested in. That is......people can put on a face to get into position in your life, and then they'll unpack their problems and move right on into your life. This is why the Bible warns against evil associations. You have to pray against the desire to be surrounded by people and learn to be on your own, accepting whomever GOD sends into your life and willing to walk away when HE says your season is up. And don't perform a role that you don't intend to stay in. If you happened to make someone laugh at your cousin's barbeque, and they invite you over, ask yourself what it is they want from you. Sometimes, they simply think you're funny, and you'd make a great comedian-friend. This is okay if they can accept the not-so-funny you, but when you have to stay within that character, you have been imprisoned. If you decide to go over, be your normal self and don't try to be the comedian because if you try to fit into their definition of you, you'll never be able to escape it without a fight.

<u>REDEFINING YOUR ROLE</u>

You're going to find that as GOD elevates you, your role is often changed and has to be redefined. This is why the characters in your story will often change. That best friend who you love so dearly today may not know or like the transformed you. With GOD, we have to always expect change for HE is always changing us for the better. The person you are today is not necessarily who you'll be tomorrow. Today you may be highly emotional and needy, calling everyone around you when a problem arises, but tomorrow, you may be healed of this behavior and confident within yourself. And sometimes, people will try to take you back to the 'you' they can relate to.

You're going to be changed, so expect it. Our stories often take turns that we didn't see coming. No one could have told me that I would be a graphic designer. I'd planned to be so many things in life, but it was GOD who shed light on who I am and how HE defines me. As I find out more about myself; I expect to change more because I am shedding the dead skin of who I thought I was and embracing the renewed and restored character that I am. I have learned so much about me, and I want to say that I know fully who I am today, but GOD just keeps on surprising me with more, so I am looking in faith for more and more revelations.

Sometimes when our roles change, everything and everyone

around us has to change. Let's say you're a man and your best friend's name is Raymond. He has been truly a wonderful friend to you in your hour of struggle, and you plan to keep him around for a lifetime. The two of you have been there for one another through thick and thin, but one day, Raymond gets elevated by GOD. He is doing so many wonderful things, and you see that he doesn't talk about people anymore, he doesn't complain too much anymore, and he doesn't gamble anymore. These were the things that connected the two of you together, but now, when you talk to him, he's different. You try to talk about your old friend Jake, and Raymond doesn't want to hear it. He reminds you that he no longer engages in this type of behavior. You start complaining about some lady cutting you off on the highway, and again, Raymond doesn't want to hear it, but instead, he cuts you off and reminds you that he doesn't like to speak negatively. He begins, instead, to talk to you about opportunities in real estate, his new position at church, and a few business ideas that he has. You ask him to accompany you to the casino, and he reminds you that he is now a man of GOD, and he doesn't gamble. Now, you're mad at Raymond because you feel like he is destroying your friendship, trying to be who he is not. Who are you to say who he is or who he isn't? Believe it or not, this situation is very common in elevation. Raymond got elevated, and his thoughts became higher and now; his friends can no longer relate to him. This will undoubtedly end the friendship, but it doesn't mean that Raymond is bad and needs to be humbled. This is one of the things I have heard with people so much, and it truly irritates me. Someone will tell me about a friend who, basically, has been elevated, and they'll go on and on about why they think this person is bad, and needs to be knocked off their high-horse. I've even heard that said about me, but in truth, people change. GOD elevates us, and we cannot burden anyone with the responsibility of fitting into our definition of them. That's a yoke, and you don't want to be found trying to yoke up the children of GOD.

How does GOD define you? You'd be amazed at how amazing you are in HIM. The secret is discovering the hidden parts of HIM and searching out the heart of GOD with vigor. These are our blessed places, and these are the only paths we have to reach our blessed places. We have all re-defined ourselves, in one way or another, but GOD defines us and helps us to rediscover who we really are in HIM.

People often say that when they are elevated, they won't change; but the truth is....you will never be elevated without changing first. A change has to be made before you can step into a new place. GOD will always refine you so that you can redefine you. Never ever get comfortable in what you know and where you are. Keep your mental bags packed and always be ready to go to the next level. It is common to arrive in places of pure peace and comfort and just want to stay there, but it takes a hard step forward to say that the devil is a liar. We can speak it all day, but is it showing in your life or has what the enemy spoke over you become your reality? At one point in my life, the devil defined me as a whore, a filthy soul, a foolish woman, a brawling woman, a depressed woman, and a woman anchored down by all kinds of hurt. I was broken, and this was my definition because it was what I displayed in my life, but when GOD began to change me, I found my definition to be a lie. What I'd told myself and what I'd been called were the characteristics of the character that I'd become, but it wasn't who I was, nor is it who I am. At first, I kept retreating back to what I knew, but it took a hard step forward, determination, and just crying out to GOD to be carried from that broken place before I discovered Tiffany, which means, "manifestation of GOD." Suddenly, my definition changed, and I redefined who I was; GOD simply showed me how HE'D defined me all along. I found that how I was in my broken state displayed characteristics of who I really am; I'd just been perverted.

Your goal is to find out who you are. That's not just your name, but it is who you really are in CHRIST. Don't get caught up in someone's definition of you. There are so many people who will gather around you and love you in your state of brokenness, but I dare you to come out and be blessed beyond recognition, and watch how fast these characters exit your story and talk about you. They will have to try to find a way to forgive you because you offended them when you went outside of their definition of you. Don't believe me? I dare you to let GOD define you so that you can redefine yourself. I dare you to find your successful place and watch how even family members disassociate themselves from you and talk horribly about you because you had the nerve to be blessed when they'd called you cursed! Watch and see how so many of your closest friends get away from you because you had the nerve to ruin that friendship by becoming unrecognizable. I've lived it, and I've met so many men and women who have lived this. When you come outside of how someone defines you, you will literally TICK THEM OFF! That's why they'll keep trying to remind you of the old dead and buried you, the one whom they can relate to, but they never want to embrace this new character, changed and holy, who is standing before them. That's when your dearest friends will resurface as some of your greatest enemies. Did you think that Satan sowed those tares amongst the wheat so that they could grow up and hold holy hands together? No way! He sowed them because he wanted to condemn the entire harvest.

Get up and change your role. Take off those dirty rags and step into the whole you. I come across so many people who keep on talking about what they will be one day and what they are called to be one day, but who you are is who you are; get up and be that today. Change just doesn't drop in anyone's lap; it has to be pursued and embraced. Change will never chase you down because change is an act of will. Are you willing to wear the royal garments that GOD has for you? Are you ready to surprise a nation by standing up and being everything they said you weren't? Are you ready to disappoint some people by breaking out of their definitions of you? If you're ready, say you're ready and stand in your change. It takes 17-21 days to break a habit. That means, starting today, you need to move forward in who you are and keep on doing it. Within 17-21 days, or shortly thereafter, old ways won't find their places in you anymore. Keep praying them off now; sometimes old ways are just demons of old that have enjoyed inhabiting your family from generation to generation, and these demons, when evicted, do try to come back with seven demons more evil than themselves. You have to make up your mind that they are locked out for good. Don't default back to the "buried" you. Default back to who you really are, how GOD has defined you from the start, and always pray that HE protects you and binds up any and every demonic spirit that has held you captive or has even dared to put its hands or mouth on you. Ask HIM to send it to the pit until the day of Judgment and bind it there. What you're doing is saying to that demon that it has been evicted, and it can't even come near you anymore!

<u>REDEFINING THE ROLES OF OTHERS</u>

One of the stories you'll find in many of my writings is my testimony about a cousin of mine. There was a point in my life I perceived as low, and I was on my own (in the natural) for the first time in my life. A cousin of mine would come by my house and help me with the things I couldn't do for myself. He was truly a huge blessing because a lot of the things I could not lift, he'd come by and pick up for me. He told me over and over again to not try to lift that stuff, but to call him when I needed help. Sometimes, I was stubborn because I tried to be Ms. Independent, but other times, I knew I had to call him whether I wanted to or not. He'd come by my house and cut my grass twice a week without me asking, and I refused to let him go away unpaid. I would give him my last, even though I was in the midst of foreclosure, my car note was past due; I was expecting the repo man at any day, and I was too heavy in the heart to stay at work. So, when they asked for volunteers to go home, I went home because I just wanted to be in a peaceful place. This cousin did not want me to pay him. He would contest, protest and go on and on, and I'd tell him that if he didn't take that money, I was coming to his house, and I'd put it in his mailbox. He'd finally give in, but I could see it bothered him because he just wanted to help. The moral of this story is...even at my lowest point, I did not use anyone. A friend of mine said I could move into her apartment, and I'd just buy a blow-up mattress and sleep on the floor, and I did for a while.

She didn't really ask for rent; she just said to give her what I could. I started giving her more than what she was paying for rent. Why is that? Because I did not want to use her. Why am I telling this story? I defined people as blessings and I wanted to be a blessing in return. I never went in with expectation, and I never tried to take advantage of a person. It was not and is not in my nature. Because of this, GOD blessed me greatly.

What's the point? Review how you define the people in your life. Name some of the people who are closest to you and ask yourself what is their role in your life. I have met so many people (even Christians...) that have a devil in their midst, and they call on this devil to deal with other devils. It might be that crazy cousin Junebug whom they have absolutely no association with. They'd occasionally give him a few bucks, hang out with him maybe once a year and just try to keep the lines of communication open. One day, somebody with a devil would challenge them, and they'd be infuriated, scared, or intimidated. That's when they'd pick up their phones and call ole Junebug, knowing good and well that Junebug served 15 years in prison for slicing up a man, and he won't hesitate to go back. They'd call him up, crying and hysterical, and before you know it, Junebug has loaded his gun or tied his machete to the back of his bicycle, and he's on his way. Of course, these people are wrong; that's evil! Rather than trying to bring him to CHRIST, they kept him on standby to handle other devils. People like this use other people as tools.

How we define others will determine if we are allowed or prohibited from entering our blessed places. If your purpose in someone's life is not to be a blessing to that person, you are operating as a user, and GOD won't bless this mentality. Even for the people who are teaching you, you ought to be a blessing in return. Never take something without being willing to give. One thing I have found is that users usually have problems with their finances. Now, that's not to say that everyone who has financial problems are users because many of them are simply climbing their GOD-given ladders. Nevertheless, many souls have adapted to this practice, and they don't realize how wrong it is. They don't realize how their ways are directing lack into their presence. When you come across a man or woman of GOD, always be willing to sow.

Again, review everyone in your life and ask yourself, "How do I see this person? How do I see that person? What are their roles in my life? What is my expectation of them? You'd be amazed at your answers and how they have affected your current financial situation. Go into every situation looking to be a blessing. A person who is a blessing pours out blessings and is always full of blessings because as soon as they pour out, GOD refills them. Some people ask, "What if I'm financially in a bind, and my friend has more money than me? Isn't it only right that she help me out until I get on my feet?" No, this is the mindset of poverty. To come out of poverty, a rich man doesn't come along and drop a load of money on you; but to get where he is, he can drop a load of knowledge on you. It's your choice what you do with that knowledge. If he supports you in your lack, he will have to continue supporting you because you will always see him as having more, therefore, having a greater responsibility in the friendship than you. But, in truth...if lack greets you, sow a seed into anointed ground. This is how you break the chains of poverty. And don't just sow a $50 seed, hoping to get $500 in return. You never look for that blessed man or woman to bless you back...instead; you look to the hills from whence cometh your help; your help cometh from the LORD. One of the examples I wrote in a previous book was the example of a man who has a net worth of $50,000 who has a friend with a net worth of $5,000,000. The man who has $50,000 may slyly give 10% of what he has to his friend. He may, for example, go out and buy a gift that cost $5,000, and he'd be sure to leave that price tag on it, reminding his friend that he's just paid 10% of what he has to be a blessing. Now, he awaits his friend's move. He expects and hopes his friend will give him a gift valued at 10% of his earnings, so he looks for a gift valued at $500,000. Was his gift given in love? No way! He understood that his friend could be a huge blessing to him if he was willing to give a small gift. Now, his motives are evil, which means his heart is evil; but he fully understands the measure of sowing and reaping. Should the millionaire friend give him a gift valued at $5,000, he'd be more than angry because along with his gift was the yoke of expectation.

This means don't give a little looking to get a lot in return...not to a person anyway. Be a blessing because you want to be a blessing and look for GOD to bless you in return. Blessings are attracted to blessings.

I have truthfully met so many wonderful people of GOD who have all grasped the message behind being a blessing, and we've tried to bless each other's socks off. Blessings are a continuous flow, and because we see one another as people who deserve to be blessed, we get blessed. And I have truthfully seen these people prosper. Poverty is a mindset, and one of its characteristics is using people for selfish gain. When one tries to measure what someone else has against what they have and tries to drain them accordingly, their finances begin to seep out because they are using a wile of the devil. Of course, many of the people bound with this mindset don't know this truth, and this is why we have to reveal it to them, offense or no offense.

Define people as GOD defines them. Look for the heart of the man and see how you can be a blessing. Not a financial blessing, unless GOD leads otherwise, but see how you can just help. The greatest gift to give someone isn't money or things, but it is wisdom. Wisdom is like a river that will quench their thirst from here on out, but giving physically only feeds the right-now need. When I learned how to be a friend, I started charging folks for services. That sounds backwards, right?

Well, it isn't. I am blessed ground, and I know it; therefore, I am robbing them from an opportunity to be blessed every time I acted outside of my character. I wasn't created to be used of man; I was created to be used of GOD. It may sound off to some, but for those that have come so far in CHRIST, you will know exactly what I mean. By feeding into a person using you, when you know you are anointed; you are actually causing a curse to ride upon that person's wallet and their lives because they are doing it with selfish motives, and this mindset is never blessed! What happens is....they go out and sow into what they want: hairdos, men, women, clothes, and so on. But, they know that they can call kindhearted you to give to them, so they don't consider that they have acted as a minus sign for your life, which means they are acting against you. Remember, GOD said that HE will bless them that bless you and curse them that curse you. So, the LORD looks around the believer (you) to see where the enemy is crouching, and HE finds him crouching in the heart of your dependent friend. The LORD watches them as they sow their seeds into wicked ground and then come back to you to act again as a minus sign. Now, you have to remember; GOD delivered you from poverty, and if HE sees it anywhere near you trying to attach to you, HE will send a refining fire upon you. This refining fire causes anything that is unlike HIM to rise to the top, and it will be poured away from you. This is when they find themselves going through lack behind lack, situation behind situation because they were attaching their lack to you; thus, cursing you. Lack is a curse and poverty is a curse, but it is NOT the portion of the believer! This is why you have to learn to say "no" to folks. Let them get mad, let them speak evil, let them do whatever they see necessary to deal with your "no." GOD taught me to stop saying "yes" to people who HE'S said "no" to. Because in saying "yes," I was agreeing to act as their god. They no longer had to go to HIM to be blessed; all they had to do was come to a person who was blessed. You might think, "Well, there are so many people whom GOD has obviously said "no" to because they don't have this or that!" That's not true at all. Even in their lack; ask them, GOD constantly says "yes." HE keeps on supplying their needs. The only difference between them and you is...you may see the money and the possessions surrounding you, whereas they keep getting blessed from all around. Their faith is being built up so they are in processing. Never interrupt this process. In other words, stop cursing people by trying to be a blessing and sowing into their mindsets. I understand that you just want to be a blessing and when you see the opportunity to be a blessing that counts in the life of someone; it's almost irresistible, but understand that GOD loves being the provider, and we can't rob HIM of this. Do you remember when you refused to do right by HIM? You knew that HE heard your prayers, and HE watched you go through the worst of the worst, yet HE wouldn't move because you wouldn't be still. **HE shares HIS glory with no man.** Anyhow, during this time, you may have lost a lot and went through a lot with no help from man. This forced you to redefine who you were and redefine your relationships because you wanted to know what you were doing wrong to cause yourself to be in this situation. You began to cry out to the LORD and humble yourself. This was your training to trust HIM. When someone else is going through their training, don't you dare intervene! Your role is not to come in and be a supplier; your role is to step in and show yourself as a testimony! But, it is human nature to want to mother something or someone. Stop it! FATHER knows best!

Pay attention to that little boy in your neighborhood, for example, that you ask to help you bring your groceries into the house. How are you blessing him? A few dollars and a "thank you?" That's not a blessing; that's a payment. Try blessing him with what he needs. For example, have you assessed his situation? Maybe he needs uniforms for school, and his parents can't afford them. You keep on sowing into his wants, but you know nothing about his need. Don't see him as your grocery

boy. See him as an opportunity to glorify the LORD.
Sometimes, you ought to just get out and bless folks for no
reason; with nothing expected. Pray on it first so you'll know
where GOD will allow you to sow. Sometimes, it's good to just
go out and buy some groceries (non perishable items) and take
them out to your local homeless shelter. Sometimes it's good to
just go out and look for someone to bless. Ask the LORD to
speak clearly to you as to whom to bless. Sometimes to break
yourself out of a situation, you simply need to get out and sow
a seed, especially if you have a problem defining people as
suppliers. You need to sow yourself out of this mindset. If you
meet a man or woman who has more money than you, don't
think about how they can benefit you; ask yourself how you can
be a blessing to them. It's kind of like the American motto:
don't ask yourself what your country can do for you; ask
yourself what you can do for your country. Change that around
and make it blessed! Don't ask yourself what someone can do
for you; ask yourself what you can do for someone else! Act
like a blessing, think like a blessing, and you will be blessed.

Redefine the roles of the characters in your story. For example,
that person whom you like to dump on, stop seeing them as
your personal toilet, but call them up to just tell them the
blessed news. I had a few people who would call me ONLY
when they were down and out, but I had to see it online or hear
it from someone else that they'd been blessed. I had to shut
that down because I realized what my role was in their story; I
was that piece of porcelain furniture that was located in the
bathroom of their hearts. After dumping off on me, they'd flush
me off the line and go on living. I wouldn't hear from them
again until they were full of mess, and they needed to release.
That wasn't and isn't who I am, so I resigned from that role. I
started seeing these people calling and I just did not feel like
being dumped on, so I let the voice-mail deal with them. It's
okay to have a friend to talk to when you're down and out, but
call them when your skies are blue as well. If you just need

someone to talk to; CHRIST is listening. Define your friends as friends because when we dump on one another, oftentimes we ruin the day for one another. You never want to be the tool that Satan uses to disable someone else, for example, from preaching today because they are heavy about your situation. Some situations have to be taken directly to GOD and left there. The issue is, people don't trust GOD; so they take these situations to other people and cast them upon them, when CHRIST said to cast your burdens upon HIM. Then these people get heavy, and you feel better. Why? Because you just threw a load of mess on them. And oftentimes, with married folks, we go and dump this mess off on our spouses and then wonder why he or she is heavy. That burden was supposed to be cast upon CHRIST. It's too heavy for you, and it's too heavy for me.

We can't just talk about people needing to redefine who we are when we refuse to review and redefine how we see people. Stop placing people in boxes and thinking they can't go outside of these boxes. That's why so many kids get grown and disassociate themselves from their parents. They know that their parents' perception of them is limited, and it is boxing them in to expectation. People like to say how horrible a person is when they don't have a relationship with their parents, but they don't ask the necessary question: Why don't these people have relationships with their parents? For the ones I have met, I found it was because their parents had tunnel vision when it came to them. They'd defined them as broken, never being able to rise above lack, sin, and a certain level of intelligence. Their parents imprisoned them in their own hurts, and they had to break out of it in order to grow.

If you change how you assign the characters or define the characters in your story, you'll systematically change the story itself. Your story will be told as GOD intended it to be told if you will only stay in HIS will no matter what. In addition, when you redefine the characters, you cause the wrong people to flee from you because in righteousness, anyone who is in the wrong place in your life is in the wrong place at the wrong time! This is when you will see who loves you and who loves the character they've assigned you to be.

THE PROPS, COSTUMES AND FURNITURE OF YOUR STORY

What are the props in our stories? The props are usually defined as anything on the set of a movie or a play, other than the costumes and the furniture. Our props are our surroundings and the things in it. Where you live is a location that is surrounded by props, your home is full of props, and your job has its fair share of props.

The Props: There may be a medicine bottle sitting on your dresser. The doctor said that you had one thing or the other, and he decreed and declared (in an intellectual way) that you'd need this medicine for the rest of your life. So now, it is a part of your scene, and you take it faithfully. If you can't find that medicine bottle, you don't know how to act and you forget your lines. That medicine has become a part of your story, and now you don't feel like there are many pages left in you without it. Remember in Isaiah 53:5, the WORD declared you healed, so now you have two scripts to read from: you have the script that your doctor gave you, and you have the scripture that the LORD gave you. Nevertheless, because you feel the symptoms, and you have witnessed some attacks from within your body, you believe and receive the doctor's script. Anyone who dares to tell you anything differently, you rebuke them; but you have yet to rebuke the words that came from that doctor's mouth. So, now medication is a part of your story. This is a great example of a prop.

Your props are any and everything that you feel has to be a part of your story. Your cell phone is a prop, your Bible is a prop, and your computer is a prop. Your props can be good or bad. A great prop is the Bible, and it's even greater when you actually open it and read it. The more you utilize it, the better your story reads. A bad prop would include pornography, drugs, alcohol, and so on. Your props can affect your life drastically because they do more than influence your life; often props control the lives of people. Even a prop that could be utilized for good can be utilized for evil.

Be prayerful about the props in your story because they just may change the title of your book and the characters in your life. People who have evil props tend to be surrounded by evil people and all things evil.

Makeup: Your makeup isn't necessarily the makeup you wear on your face, but it is the face that you put on for others. Think about the scripture where the LORD told us not to disfigure our face when we are fasting. There are people who want you to know what's going on in their lives, so they transform their face to speak a message. Have you ever run into someone who always needs money and always needs sympathy? And you hate to go to the store and see them because you know the pity party is about to begin, and they are the host? As soon as you try to avoid them, they spot you and disfigure their face as they approach you. Now, before they saw you, they were laughing and walking with no problem, but the minute they saw you, all of a sudden, they are walking with a limp, and they look pitiful. They approach you and they wait for that infamous, "How are you doing?" Once you ask this question, they go on to tell you how their blood pressure has been sky high, their diabetes is eating them up, their light bill is due and their children are running them crazy. Before you leave, they either ask for some money, or they ask for your phone number (so they can call you and ask for some money.) They put on their makeup, and they auditioned for a part in your heart. In the pity section, that is.

People put on all kinds of makeup before engaging with other people. That man who wants to lie with you may put on a face of love. He looked deeply into your eyes, and you could have sworn that you saw a spark of love there, but in truth, what you saw was hell hiding behind his pupils. Once you've given in again and again; all of a sudden, you don't see that spark anymore, and it's hard for you to reconcile the fact that there just wasn't any love there from the beginning. This is when people start looking for villains. Someone has to be messing with his head, in your eyes. In truth, he dressed himself in a costume, packed on his makeup, and put on an Oscar worthy performance.

What about that woman who smiled at you and pretended to be so deeply in love with you? She gazed at you like no woman has ever gazed at you before. It felt like she was staring down into your soul, and no man could separate you from her. An alimony payment and a restraining order later, you discover that when she was staring in your eyes, she was looking at her own reflection. Her interest in you had nothing to do with love, but had everything to do with the fact that she felt like you financially met the requirements of the character she wanted in her life. She didn't want you; she wanted your bank account number, so she married you, gave you children and then; all of a sudden, she wants a divorce. She wore her makeup and her costume like a perfectionist, and her act deserved a standing ovation.

Every character in your story will come wearing the truth or wearing makeup. Ask the LORD to rain down on them and wash away their masks, and you will find that some of the characters in your story wasn't at all who they appeared to be.

Costumes: Our costumes are what we wear. It is what we feel defines the character we are, or the character we are pretending to be. The costume that a man or woman selects will tell you much about the character that's wearing it. People can lie and pretend to be something that they are not, but a lot of times, you don't need discernment to pick up on who they really are. You simply need a pair of working eyes. A woman who tries to court you can easily say that she's a decent, GOD-fearing woman, and that she will be faithful to you all of your life; but, her costume says "loose." She wears the costume of a harlot for a reason. She wasn't lying with her clothes. She was lying with her mouth. Nevertheless, because she wanted a role in her life, she put on an act and hoped that you'd hire her. Then, there is that friend who you let come to your house. Let's say, for example, that you are married. This friend likes to visit you and wear her "hooker" clothes to your house. She looks like she's wearing lingerie, and she likes to walk past your husband. That's just her and she's harmless, right? Wrong. Her costume will tell you a story that you don't want to read. Even if she's a humble and sweet girl, there is a reason that she's dressing like a night walker. Women often say, for example, "Well, I've known her for years, and she has never tried to mess with any of the boyfriends I've had." What these characters don't understand is: Maybe the boyfriends they had were not worth, in their minds, destroying the friendship over. Dare to get someone who's worth it, and you'll find her doing everything in her power to get him. If one walked up to a prostitute, and she was asking for $75 to lie with her, do you think she'd accept $10? It wasn't worth it and she'll walk away, right after telling that person a piece of her mind. Well, this is the same thing. If someone comes around you wearing a costume, believe what the clothes are saying about the character.

In addition, be careful with the costumes you put on your body. Sometimes, other characters have worn these costumes; and you freely put them on, thinking that nothing is wrong with them. But, the Israelites had to destroy the cursed things once they won a war and wanted to loot the land. GOD would allow them to take certain things sometimes, but other times, in some countries; amongst some people, GOD would require that they destroy everything there. Why is that? Because of the curse that was attached to that place. It had to be consecrated. Pay attention. If your promiscuous cousin gave you a pair of pants, you may start to feel a fire welding up inside of you. All of a sudden, you go from being a good girl to buying whips and chains, and you can't understand why. It's because everything that is attached to her holds her DNA. Do you remember that when the LORD told the Apostles that if a land didn't receive them, to shake off the very dirt of that place from their feet as a testament against them? That dirt was cursed along with that place. When we wear clothing, did you know that we shed cells in those clothes, and no amount of washing can get rid of them? It's okay to say "no" when people offer you clothing. Can you consecrate it? Pray over it and let the LORD deliver the clothing? Nothing is impossible for GOD, but I would definitely pray before they brought it over and ask the LORD if I could accept it. I would ask HIM to stand in the way and not let me accept the clothing, if HE didn't want me to have it.

I have even met a few people who had clothing from their past, and they found that every time they wore them, they would feel "sinful." After praying, the LORD revealed that they had to get rid of the clothing because it was a part of their history. A good example would be underwear that you wore to fornicate in. Ladies, sometimes, your costumes will keep you from being found by your GOD-appointed husbands. Do you really believe that GOD will send this man to marry you when you are still sporting the bracelet that the last man gave you? Do you really believe that GOD will send HIS son to find you when you are found wearing underwear that you have fornicated in? Even though you're trying to live right now, you have to get rid of your past in its entirety. You can't section it off and keep what you believe to be harmless. Guys, those old photos of you and your ex-girlfriends will keep you from finding your GOD-appointed wives because you're still holding on to history and hoping to merge it with your future, and it's just not happening.

For those of you who are married and finding yourself constantly divided in your home, look for what's dividing you. Sometimes, it is something as small as a ring that an ex gave you. That stuff has to go! It is a part of your history, and history should be left in the past!

Furniture: Furniture is just what it says, furniture. Our furniture can and does play a role in our stories. Let's go back to what's given to you. Let's say that cousin Sherry gave you a mattress set. She said it was like new, and because you'd just moved into your apartment, you saw this as a blessing. Now, you got all kinds of madness going on in your apartment, and you can't understand why. Why all of a sudden you feel the need to sleep with this and that person? Could it be what's in that mattress? Indeed, even though some may beg to differ, the truth is: you can't take anything from everyone. Cousin Sherry may have been fornicating or committing adultery all over that mattress, and now your usually faithful husband has wandering eyes and wants to try different things and different people. GOD told the Israelites to destroy that stuff for a reason.

Sometimes, it is better to have no furniture and to be patient with GOD, knowing that one day you can purchase something new, than it is to accept something used and abused by someone else. You can throw anointing oil all over that new couch or that bad, but it won't change what happened there. Patience is a virtue. That's for real! ***"But the fruit of the Spirit is love, joy, peace, longsuffering, gentleness, goodness, faith, meekness, temperance: against such there is no law."***

(Galatians 5:22-23)

I underlined "longsuffering," which is another word for patience, and I underlined "faith" because you have to believe GOD will provide for you. Be patient with GOD. I can testify that when my husband and I first moved to Florida; we didn't have a dime to our name, so we couldn't afford to get furniture. I was used to being in bondage with monthly notes, so I proposed that we go and get some furniture on credit. I was eager to sit down on a couch or lie down on a bed, but my husband wasn't having it. He said that if we could not afford to pay for it in cash, we weren't going to have it. I was frustrated! I was angry and I put up many arguments, but he'd lie down on that air mattress and ignore me. Finally, after a couple of months, we purchased a bed and a mattress. We'd gone to the store previously and the bed frame was $299, but when we went back to buy it, it was on sale for $199! Yes, that was GOD! So we got the bed, purchased a mattress, and slowly; but surely, our apartment began to fill up. It took over a year to completely fill it, but once it was full, we had money to toy with and money to save. We had no monthly bills except utilities and rent. Patience paid off, and I thanked my husband for not listening to that recently freed girl who wanted to return to bondage. People did offer to give us furniture, but I declined because I know what grown folks do on their furniture. Be careful what furniture comes into your story because furniture that belonged to someone else has its own story to tell.

Anyone can argue that we don't know what happened on those new couches or new mattresses that we want to purchase, but what they can't argue with is the truth that we can pray and ask the LORD to lead us in our selections. A little bit of faith can make a whole world of difference!

What's the conclusion?

Everyone and everything in your life is a part of your story. What story is it telling in your life? We can pretend that these things don't affect our lives, but everything that surrounds us, represents us, and what we allow to represent us, speaks to others about the GOD we serve. How can you say that you are saved and sanctified if your clothes say otherwise? How can you properly represent the LORD if your makeup represents darkness?

To be blessed and stay blessed, you have to set up the scene in the right way. This requires patience, love and the desire to please GOD above man. When you decide to tell your story the right way, you have no choice, but to offend the man who wants to add the wrong scenes and characters to your book. Your life is assigned to you by GOD; set it up right so that you'll attract the right audience.

FICTION OR NONFICTION

How dare someone ask this question, right? Your life is nonfiction, even though you've dealt with your fair share of lies, false people, and misconceptions. In truth, most people live fictitious lives because the average man and woman does not know who they really are, so they morph into a duplicate of who they want to be. Look around and you'll see carbon copies of celebrities walking around. Listen and you'll hear the same ole way of talking coming from different lips. When we do not know our true identities, we go shopping for personalities, styles, and dreams we feel happy with. Ask 80% of children what they want to be when they grow up, and they will say they want to be doctors. This is their parents' dream, and this is what they have been fed, so they proudly proclaim it and then look at their parents to see that heart-warming smile that lets them know that they've answered well. As they grow older, many of them discover that they are disgusted and even become nauseous at the sight of blood, so a medical doctor is out of the question. That's when many say that they want to be a psychiatrist or a psychologist. They're still doctors, but they don't have to deal with needles, blood, surgery, and all that icky stuff. By the time the child is between 15-18 years of age, they've had another change of heart. Now, in discovering more about the different fields and the time required to accomplish these goals, they settle on what they feel is right for their lives.

Mommy and Daddy just have to suck it up and deal with it. As children, they presented this character for their parent's amusement, but as they got older, they decided they wanted to be another character. Sometimes, they discover who they are, and other times; they like who someone else is, so they morph into that character.

Growing up, I can remember when certain celebrity musicians would be at the top of the charts. Most children and many adults began to mimic their dress and their hair. When Michael Jackson was at the top of the charts, I remember seeing so many kids wearing Thriller jackets and sporting Jheri curls. As rap and hip hop came on the scene, the clothing and the speech began to change more and more. Suddenly, the pants started falling off the rumps and whatever artist was on top was mocked more than anything. When a rapper named Snoop Dog was "in," just about every young guy was walking like him, dressing like him, and speaking like him. Then, there was the Master P era where little boys reached back into their throats to mimic his sounds. Nowadays, the fads are becoming more and more demonic. It is the in-thing now for kids to tattoo up their necks, and I'm pretty sure it has something to do with one of the artists, but because I don't listen to secular music anymore, I can't specifically point out who this fad has originated from. But, having seen magazine articles, Internet articles and commercials, I can assure that a rapper by the name of Lil Wayne is behind the excessive tattooing. Then again, I could be wrong.

These children and adults start to become the character that they idolize and the sad part is, people see this word "idolize" and don't pay attention to the root of it. To idolize someone is to set them up as an idol in your heart, and this is absolute sin. No idolaters will enter Heaven! That is the WORD of GOD!

GOD said to "guard your heart, for it is a wellspring of life."

That's in Proverbs 4:23, but the heart of man is open for all kinds of wickedness and whatever a man is fed, he will become. When he is fed wisdom, he will become wise; but when he is fed foolishness, he will become foolish.

You have to get back to your GOD-assigned roles and stop assuming the roles Satan has drawn up for his script. Satan's script for you always ends in you dying prematurely and going to hell. A good writer will tell a story, bring a little drama in the story, introduce a hero, and save the people with this hero. Afterward, the villain is killed or imprisoned, and the people live happily ever after....that is until someone decides to make a sequel. Satan's story doesn't go that way. His story starts off with you falling into a little drama, being introduced to sin and living happy in that sin. Then, the "big scene" comes where you die in your sin, but the story doesn't end there. It plays on and on for eternity with you being in the pits of hell, crying out in agony, while he does the same thing with your children and their children's children. Who wants that role? Most people like happy endings.

What character are you playing? On average, most people alive are playing someone. If you say that you have not taken on the role of someone else, then let me ask you this way; what is your role in life and who are you in CHRIST? What are your talents? What is your GOD-given name? Not the name your mother gave you, but the name that GOD calls you? Paul was Saul; Simon Peter was Simon Barjona; Jacob was Israel and so on. The changing of the name represented the changing of the life and the transitioning from the dead man to the eternal man. Yes, you may walk with your natural name all of your life and still be changed, but the point is; who are you in HIM? Your name is not what your parents called you. *"He that hath an ear, let him hear what the Spirit saith unto the churches; To him that overcometh will I give to eat of the hidden manna, and will give him a white stone, and in the stone, a new*

name written, which no man knoweth saving he that receiveth it" (Revelations 2:17).
If you don't know who you are, you will assume the role of another character, and you will have to walk in purpose, seeking the Word of GOD to have this character to shed away from you like dead skin. The more you walk in CHRIST, the more you will discover about yourself.

But, many of us get stuck in our own personal goals. We travel down the road of righteousness, looking for our GOD-appointed assignments. We search out HIS heart, and we witness many miracles, signs, and wonders along the way, and this is where we get comfortable. We're going up the steps, but once we have arrived at a place close to HIM that we are satisfied with; we take off our shoes and get comfortable right there on the steps. Death is always on our heels trying to take us prematurely, but as long as we are searching out the heart of GOD and walking in purpose, death has to stay behind us. When we stop, however, and decide that we have come far enough, we are no longer in purpose, but we begin to reside in disobedience. This gives death the ability to catch up and begin to unload sickness, poverty, insanity and every other cursed thing upon us. Jonah had a choice: live in purpose or die in the belly of that whale. He chose to live and declare the works of the LORD. As human beings, we tend to arrive at a certain place and think we have journeyed far enough because we have come further than the people we know. Many times, those same people will criticize you because they feel like you're going too far. "You're so heavenly-minded that you're no earthly good!" I'm sure you've heard that quote before, especially if you have went outside of the perimeters of man's limited understanding. So, you stop right there and praise the LORD, even though the LORD is calling you to continue deeper and deeper into HIS heart. No one recognizes you anymore, and they think that something is wrong with you because you are not the same person who they knew. That's because the person, they knew was a fictitious character, and now you are becoming who GOD has called you to be; peculiar, not familiar. The dead you has begun to shed, and it's not a comfortable place. We want to get up and go back to the familiar character we'd learned to play and many do go back, but when you really love the LORD, you know to keep going.

The ones that continue to go forward often find themselves losing friends, and their relationships with their families become more and more strained. They find themselves alone and wondering if something really is wrong with them. Have they made the right choice? They cry out to GOD, and HE confirms that HE is doing a work in them. Some people want the work to stop because they miss having friends and family in their lives. And then there are the ones that don't care if they serve HIM alone or with a crowd....it's all about HIM and their life reflects their love, loyalty and dedication to HIM. These are the characters who live long, healthy lives and find who they really are. They shed the dead skin of their fictitious character, and the true person emerges.

What are you? Who are you? You have to go into GOD to discover the truth about your identity, and this will help you to embrace the next chapter of your life. This is when stress and anxiety can't find any place in our hearts to unpack their bags, so it has to find somewhere else to live. Who are you? This is what you need to be asking the LORD, but you won't find who you are until you have discovered who GOD is. You are not GOD, but HE created us to discover ourselves, our purposes, our mates, our successes, our health, and every good thing in HIM. As we journey further into the perfect knowledge of GOD, the whole picture begins to form, and we even discover why we went through what we've gone through, why certain people had to be removed from our walks and why we love to do what we love to do. There is joy in discovering the whole heart of GOD.

You choose whether you want to live a fictitious lifestyle or a life of truth. When you stand before the LORD, if you are found a liar, you cannot enter Heaven. That's the truth. Your pastor cannot tell you who you are, but he or she can and should point you to GOD for that answer. Go to church, read your Bible, but above all things, pray and serve GOD in obedience. Do your part and refuse to let sin be a part of your story. Yes, we are all sinners saved by grace, and we all fall short of the glory of GOD, but here's the difference between a sinner and a redeemed man: A sinner lives in his sin and it is found in him at any given time. Repentance is not in his immediate plans. A man redeemed by GOD strives to please the LORD; his life, walk, and speech reflects his love for the LORD and his convictions. If he should stumble, he immediately repents and continues serving the LORD because he desires to be near the heart of GOD at all times. Again, to repent does not mean to apologize to the LORD; to repent means to "turn away from" the sin and to "turn back to" GOD. This means that you avoid that sin from this day out. It does not mean that you get up and apologize to GOD, only to go back and repeat the sin and follow it up with another apology. A sinner returns to his sin like a dog returns to his vomit. This means that he'll keep going back to it, but if you love HIM, your obedience will speak louder than your mouth. *"If ye love me, keep my commandments" (John 14:15).* Anyone can say that they love the LORD, but the old adage says it best: <u>actions speak louder than words!</u>

A HORROR STORY

We have all had some periods in our lives that we have labeled "horrible." These were the times that we couldn't concentrate on living because something horrible was distracting us. It may have been hard to eat or keep food down because life presented us with a villain (a person or a situation) whose antics we had to endure. Maybe it was your boss at a particular establishment who seemed focused on making your life at work miserable, or he may have been focused on getting rid of you. Or it could have been that car of yours that just wouldn't start, and now the mechanics are asking for money that you don't have. Oftentimes, when one wrong event occurs, a series of bad events fall upon us making that time seem like a horror story. This is normal, and you can expect to be challenged from time to time.

Needless to say, there are many people who don't endure horrible <u>periods</u>, but their lives are a continuous horror story. You may look at them and think that life is so unfair to them, and you wish you could help them out. Then again, you may be the person who is living this horror story. Please understand that any horrible time for you represents a time where you can be gaining the wisdom from the situation, and at the same time glorifying the LORD.

Review the Bible and you will find that there were many situations that seemed unfair, and the men of GOD had to endure some pretty hard trials. Job is the most renowned of them all because he had to endure something that would run most of mankind crazy, yet he got through it without doing what Satan wanted him to do, and that was to curse GOD. He came out more blessed than he went in, and he came out wiser.

Nowadays, we are a very weak generation. People tend to go into an emotional tail spin when their jobs are threatened; sometimes destroying their families and taking their own lives. Take into consideration that there are job opportunities in the United States; not to mention there are endless opportunities to start and run your own businesses. Nevertheless, some people choose to let fear write their script, and they play out their dramatic scenes to perfection.

A horror story to you just may be a love story to the LORD. Many times, we endure "chastenings" that were purposed in correcting us. Other times, we endure "trials," that were purposed in testing us. And then, there are "tribulations," which are similar to "chastenings," but tribulations are periods of times when we are to go through a punishment because of disobedience. A chastening can be short-lived, but a tribulation often has an already predetermined date set by GOD that the person or persons have to endure. The Israelites, for example, had to endure a tribulation of walking 40 years in the wilderness. It is still a form of chastening since GOD did not put them away. David was chastened for having Uriah killed and sleeping with Bathsheba. His punishment was that his son with Bathsheba (firstborn) would die, and the sword would never leave his family. ***"For whom the Lord loves he chastens, and scourges every son whom he receives. (Hebrews 12:6)"***

We could say that being in the wilderness is a horror story, but it is actually a witness to GOD'S love for us. We could say that

David's punishment was extreme, but you have to understand that a punishment is not a paddling followed by a pacifier. A punishment is purposed in making us think twice about repeating the sin. It is to get us to understand that the WORD of GOD is true and to fear the LORD. Think about wild animals. A wild animal has a natural fear of man, but when man begins to feed it, it loses that fear. Animals are naturally dangerous because many of them instinctively kill to survive. The instinctive need to kill is still present even when the animal has lost its fear of humans. This puts any person who comes in contact with such an animal in grave danger. This is why many wildlife reservations warn people about feeding the animals. In many areas, they have to kill any animals that have lost their fear of man because those areas are frequented by people. Let's go back to our fear of GOD. When man is not punished, he loses his fear of GOD, and he may become bolder and bolder; even attacking the people of GOD. When we sin, we distance ourselves from the LORD, but those that stay near HIM are fenced into HIS heart. Anyone who tries to breach this fence to harm one of HIS children falls in immediate danger. A chastening is a very humbling experience, as it is intended to be. In order for man to continue to fear the LORD and to turn away from sin, punishments must be enacted.

But, why the horror stories? Why do some people live in absolute misery? Is there something they can do to come out of that horrible place and live in the blessings of GOD?

Why? The heart of man is increasingly evil and man tends to continue sinning against GOD, even though they've been warned time and time again. Let's say that you have a cousin named Jeremy that goes to church and serves on the deacon board. He reads his Bible often, and he prays every day, but his household is one of chaos. His sons keep getting arrested; his daughters keep getting pregnant out of wedlock; his wife was diagnosed with lung cancer, and the deacon himself has lost his job and is about to lose his house. That's a horror story. What's wrong? Well, take a deeper look into his life. Jeremy has been playing with fire. He has been committing adultery against his wife and against another man. You see; cousin Jeremy was sleeping with Deacon Dandridge's wife for the last few years. He nor his wife disciplined their children because they saw discipline as cruel, totally disregarding the WORD of GOD. The deacon's wife has been dealing with her issues by cursing the deacon and smoking a pack of cigarettes a day. Not to mention, they allow their sons and daughters to fornicate under their roof. Did GOD bring calamity upon the deacon? No. Deacon brought calamity upon his own house because he chose to play with sin, and he found out that a man could not take fire in his bosom and not be burned. Deacon is like many believers; he believes somewhat, but he doesn't truly believe the WORD in its entirety. He is a bi-believer, a non-believer, or he is a believer who thinks that he is exempt; but when he decided to sin, the wages of sin visited his household. Being the strongman, he opened his door to sin and sin did what sin does...it destroys a family, corrupts the mind, and represents its sender... the devil.

Is there something they can do to come out of that horrible place and live in the blessings of GOD?
Sure. Repent and obey GOD. *"If my people, which are called by my name, shall humble themselves, and pray, and seek my face, and turn from their wicked ways; then will I hear from heaven, and will forgive their sin, and will heal their land." (2 Chronicles 7:14)*

Deacon would have to get his house back in order and proclaim as Joshua proclaimed, "As for me and my house, we will serve the LORD." He can't just say it, but he has to live it.

Horror stories also become a part of our story when our flesh is trying to act in the role that GOD assigned our spirit man to.

Let's say, for example, that Sister Shanice loves to come to church and worship the LORD, but when she goes home, she is in her husband's face about his latest affair. Shanice is heartbroken and angry, and she decides to take it upon herself to correct her husband. After all, GOD is taking longer than she wants him to take. So, she's going through her husband's cell phone, cursing him, pushing him, and ridiculing him. After all this, she goes to bed and says her prayers. She asks the LORD yet again to deal with her husband and his mistress. One day, her husband gets up and decides he wants a divorce, and he wants Shanice to move out of the family home. Their arguments grow more and more intense, and his hate for her continues to bud. Is her husband wrong for the affair? Yes. So, why is sister Shanice being punished even more? Shanice's husband brought this horrible situation to her, but just like a chess game, once she discovered what was going on, it was her turn to make a move. She obviously decided that she wanted to stay in that marriage, but she wanted her husband to stop having the affair. She did the right thing initially by praying. She sinned when she decided to get in the LORD'S way and try to fix her husband herself. He needed to be taught a lesson, and Shanice decided to try on GOD'S shoes and teach him this lesson. Therefore, what GOD was reading about her life was a horror story to HIM. Initially, it was a story that had no ending, and HE wanted to add an ending to it that would glorify HIS name, but Shanice decided to add her own scenes to the story and act them out herself. She did not realize she was reading from Satan's script, and he'd designed the script for her to act up, and help her husband feel justified in his act. Her husband's cue came when Shanice confirmed the lies that he'd been told by the enemy, and when he exited the stage, unforgiveness came on the scene. At the end of this charade, Satan gave a standing ovation and every demon that was assigned to destroy that marriage took a bow. Remember this: GOD will not co-author with Satan; you are either following GOD'S will, or you are following Satan's script.

Why? Shanice decided to ignore that vengeance belongs to the LORD. Yes, she was hurting and GOD knows that she was hurting, but we are not to respond to the pain by sinning. We should always respond to the wrong by speaking the WORD of GOD and staying in an obedient and praying position. GOD will not share HIS glory with man; therefore, you can't bring sin in and expect GOD to put HIS signature on it. When you decide to fix it yourself, GOD will let you see how your results turn out and when you get tired of getting whipped around by the devil...maybe...just maybe, you will turn it over to HIM wholly and watch how HE changes the direction of that story.

Is there something they can do to come out of that horrible place and live in the blessings of GOD? Indeed. Shanice needs to humble herself and get back in a place of trusting GOD with her marriage. Rather than letting her emotions cause her to sin; she should take what she feels and cast that burden upon the LORD. She should treat her husband with kindness, remaining a chaste wife, and presenting her case to the LORD. GOD has a special script for HIS children, and HE would have either caused her husband to repent and learn to love his wife all over again, or HE would have given her husband to his sin to let him feel the impact of what it is doing to his family.

One of my horror stories came when my husband, and I started living together. He was letting a family member interfere in our marriage, and I was livid. I argued with him just about every day, and I cried more than a baby does because I was more than determined to get my marriage on track or to abandon the marriage. I constantly threatened my husband with divorce, and I began to despise him. In return, he grew closer to the person who wanted to separate us, and we would go days without speaking to one another. It was horrible. The LORD kept telling me to humble myself, but I thought that if I humbled myself, my husband would think that he "won" and he'd let this family member finally have the "power" position that she so craved. So, I continued to fight it out, pack my bags, take off my wedding ring, and look for divorce attorneys. One day, I decided to do it GOD'S way, and I started being a humble and loving wife. I talked to my husband about what was wrong, and I let him make his own mistakes. I stopped throwing dagger for dagger at the family member, and I let him see for himself what was going on. You see, initially; he thought he saw two women competing, and he didn't know what to do. He was determined to please both women, but once I began to do as the LORD commanded me, my husband's eyes began to open, and he saw the situation for what it was. I learned to love him and humble myself as a wife, and he learned what being a husband entailed. He finally chose his marriage, and nowadays; he doesn't allow anyone to come between us. He even advises his friends and family. What was my horror story? Was it what he was doing? Yes, that hurt, but the horror story began the minute that I stepped from under my husband's covering and decided to wage war against him. When the LORD told me that I was acting like a "Jezebel," that was enough to make me humble myself and get back in position. You see; a position of obedience is a warring position. Even though you look and feel weak, when you measure your actions with your pride, in truth, it takes a lot of strength to be still when you want to do otherwise.

When the LORD was reading my story, HE saw an opportunity to glorify HIS name; train my husband and I for warfare, and to bless us with the wisdom needed to help others who found themselves in similar situations. But, I saw it as an opportunity to prove that "I wasn't the one." That way of thinking was pure and undiluted pride that GOD had to deflate. The whole time that I fought, GOD let me go round for round with myself, but there came the hour when there was nothing left to squeeze out of me. I had nothing left in my idea bag, but prayer and repentance. When I realized that I wasn't representing GOD, and that it was a training experience, I stood up and did as the LORD commanded. I battled in the spirit with a fire so intense that I didn't recognize myself. It's been years now, and our marriage has never been better because I decided to let GOD be GOD and Tiffany be obedient.

Horror stories often start and end in disobedience. You can come out by simply obeying GOD and learning to take the wisdom from that situation. You don't have to continue to live in a horror story, for in all things, there is something you can take from it.

And you can change how the story ends for you and begins for your children. Many of the horrors that we live in are generational curses and mindsets. This is a hard thing to come out of because what we are taught embeds itself within the core of our hearts. It is what we know, and it is what we are accustomed to doing, but GOD created you to overcome this. Your story does not have to read like your parents' stories or your grandparents' stories. You have the opportunity to repent and ask the LORD for a changed mind so that you can stop that curse with you. Your children won't have to struggle with it if you would only overcome it for them.

Give the pen to CHRIST JESUS and watch HIM write beautiful things upon your heart. The devil lied and told you that CHRIST would change your life for the worse, and you'd have to wait to get to Heaven before you could enjoy living. In truth, GOD wants to better your life as a whole. Yes, we suffer shame, ridicule, persecution, imprisonment, physical attacks, and even death for HIS name's sake, but HE is oh-so-worth it! Nevertheless, what HE wants to write upon the tablet of your heart will make you dance, sing, understand, and believe.

It's your choice. We all know that horror stories tend to be followed by a sequel, but you don't have to wait for that devil to come back with seven demons more evil than itself when you can simply bind it and cast it into the pit. Matthew 16:19 reads,

"And I will give unto thee the keys of the kingdom of heaven: and whatsoever thou shalt bind on earth shall be bound in heaven: and whatsoever thou shalt loose on earth shall be loosed in heaven." It's your right to be free! Exercise it.

A LUST STORY

GOD is turning the pages of your life, and what does HE see? Is that you getting ready to give yourself to someone whom you have not committed yourself to as a spouse before HIM? As much as HE loves you, this is one scene that HE doesn't want to see. After all, would you like to be forced to watch your children, when they grow up, act out a porn scene? If that would enrage you, imagine how HE feels. HE can't look upon this scene because GOD cannot look upon sin, but HE knows what you've just done. Many wake up from their beds of fornication and adultery diseased, and they cry out and ask the LORD why HE allowed this to happen to them. They try to reason by saying that they've never murdered or raped anyone, so why are they condemned to premature death or a limited lifestyle just because of something as small as fornication? Again, GOD cannot look upon sin. If HE did look at you in that hour, you'd be _____ flat-lined without a remedy. So, when you decided to fornicate, you were on your own with the very devils you were serving.

Not to mention, fornication is a sin against your own body. When you decided to act out this porn scene, you must have forgotten that you asked the LORD to watch over you. We do need HIS protection, but HIS protection is in HIS will. Outside of it, you walk into HIS wrath. You probably didn't plan this scene, however. You thought you'd go and visit your boyfriend or girlfriend, and the two of you would play a game of checkers, exchange a few kisses, and you'd be on your way back home, daydreaming of the wonderful night it was. Again, you forgot something; you're wrapped in flesh. So, you head on over and things start off just as you'd planned them. The two of you laugh, play a nice game of checkers, and then you exchange a kiss, but something happens in that kiss that you didn't plan for. Your flesh woke up and started making fiery demands. Then you started reasoning within yourself, and you threw your inhibitions to the wind. After the act has been completed, conviction visits you, and you find yourself feeling like GOD doesn't want you anymore. You feel like you just can't get it right, no matter how hard you try. After all, you came there with checkers on your mind, but instead you became the game that got played. Your story went on to include an X-rated scene, and the sad part is, GOD is reading what you are living.

How does one stop fornicating? That's easy; stop placing yourself in a position where you can fornicate. The flesh is weak and willing to sin at any given moment. You should know that by now. So, if you don't want to fornicate, you can't go to his or her house or allow him or her in your house. You need to avoid being alone together; even in the car. People do park between the trees and try to repent later.

Ladies: If he's not your husband, he hasn't earned the right to be alone with you. A man will take freely whatever you give him, but what you make him earn; he will work for and appreciate. Yes, even time alone with you. Now, a nice stroll on the beach is okay because people are there, but when the LORD turns the lights off in Heaven, and the night starts to dawn upon you; the two of you should be heading your separate ways because night-time is husband-time. If he hasn't married you, don't give him the benefit of having this time alone with you. He will respect and appreciate you for this and the ones that leave you alone because of this never intended to stick around in the first place. A man who can walk away easily will eventually walk away anyway. Would you rather him walk away in the beginning of the relationship when no soul tie is established and you simply "like" him, or would you prefer to "love" him, have this heart-wrenching soul tie with him and have him leave you once you're spent?

Fellows: If she's not your wife, don't place yourself or her in a position where either one or both of you are tempted. Pay attention to the woman. If she is insisting on being alone, and does not respect your desire to respect her, chances are, she's not your wifely treasure. Your wife is a treasure, and the LORD has given you a map to her heart, but it isn't easy to find. It is found in your obedience to HIM, and any woman that calls you or tempts you into sin isn't located in the LORD. Anything that is easy isn't a treasure; it's a pleasure. If you are looking for your wife, stand your ground and insist that the two of you only see one another in public places and public settings. Believe it or not, most women, who have been sexually active and who are still bound by a soul tie or several soul ties, will label you as "weak" and leave you. This is great news! Had you slept with her, you would have become her husband illegally, and you would be responsible for providing for her (being heirs together) and living with her as a husband should. If you did not, your prayers would be hindered. (*Reference 1 Peter 3:7*)

Anytime you refuse to place yourself in a position where you can fornicate, the other person, if they are not right with GOD, will get tired of "wasting their time" with you and go on with their life. Why do some people think that this is a bad thing? When someone wrestles with their flesh, they will NEVER make a good mate. Instead, that man who couldn't wait for you, woman of GOD, will find himself burning for another woman because his lack of patience was not activated by his love for you, but his flesh. A man of the flesh does fleshly things. Instead, that woman who saw you as "weak," man of

GOD, will find herself losing respect for you more and more because she defines a "real man" as someone who sins with her, cheats on her, disrespects her, or lies to her. She's of the flesh, and this is what she's used to.

When you are found by your GOD-appointed spouses, they will be patient and loving. They will love the idea of being able to experience you for the first time on wedding night because they love the LORD. Since they love the LORD enough to honor HIM, they will love you enough to respect you, and their fear of GOD will keep them in order, not your .48 caliber pistol. You won't have to be driving around town at three in the morning, crying and wiping your eyes with their photos. Instead, you can rest peacefully, knowing that GOD sent this one to you, and divorce won't be found in your vocabulary.

What will GOD see when HE turns the page on your life tomorrow? Can you quit the unedited porno scenes so that HE can add blessings to your life's book? If you've been sexually active before, I know that it won't be easy, but prayer, and wisdom will keep you whole.

A LOVE STORY

"For God so loved the world, that he gave his only begotten Son, that whosoever believeth in him should not perish, but have everlasting life. For God sent not his Son into the world to condemn the world; but that the world through him might be saved" (John 3:16-17).

What else is there to know about love? GOD wrote a love story to us, and HE called it the Bible. In this story, we witness how man has sinned again and again against the LORD, and we witness how HE has forgiven us again and again. Then, to show HIS undying, unyielding, unlimited love for us, HE sent HIS only-begotten Son to die for us. There is no story more powerful than that one.

Now, you have a pen and your life is the paper. You are responding to HIS story with your story and how you respond will determine how your story ends. You know what HE'S done for you. You know that HE loves you. After all, HE woke you up this morning and sent you on your way. Your day may not be the best day, but you're alive in it. In each breath is the opportunity to change the way our story reads to GOD.

I remember a time in my life where I was "straddling the fence," as they say. I loved the LORD, went to church often, and prayed daily. During that time, I was talking about how good GOD has been to me, but when those challenges came my way, I was cursing like I didn't know GOD. I was ready to fight, and I was ready to do whatever it took to get me back to a state of peace. When peace finally found me, I would settle down and go back to telling people how much I love the LORD. How double-minded was I?

GOD got my attention several times after my tantrums. Where was my love for HIM at that moment, and why wasn't it strong enough to make me humble myself? I had to realize that my love for HIM had limitations, and this was evident in my actions. In times of peace, I adored HIM, but in times of war, I put HIM behind my pride. So, my book's response sounded like it came from a bipolar maniac. There was the soft-voiced, sweet, and loving girl who worshiped the LORD and then, when the fire came, this loud and aggressive character emerged that didn't say anything about the LORD. I was so hurt at seeing how I was. How could I change this? After all, I was going to church, reading my Bible, praying, and my heart did yearn for GOD. During those times, I was being tried by fire, and anytime the fire came upon me, whatever was in me rose to the surface. Those times did not come as an attack against me, they were allowed to pass through me because of what was in me. GOD wanted me to see what was still there, hiding behind the shadows of my smile and a religious front. I had to learn to pray against it and to stop working against GOD with my words and actions. It looked like a bad time in my life, but it was another love story. GOD loved and loves me so much that HE would allow me to go through fire without being destroyed! HE allowed me to be refined, as painful and uncomfortable as it was, so that what was keeping me from HIM would be exposed and removed. I learned that whenever I'm tried by fire that it is because something is lurking in my heart that GOD wants to destroy. Rather than consuming me in the fire of HIS wrath, HE allows me to be tried by the refining fire of HIS WORD, so that anything that is unlike HIM will surface. That's where my will has to come in. I have to choose what I do with what I see. *"That the trial of your faith, being much more precious than of gold that perisheth, though it be tried with fire, might be found unto praise and honour and glory at the appearing of Jesus Christ: Whom having not seen, ye love; in whom, though now ye see him not, yet believing, ye rejoice with joy unspeakable and full of glory: Receiving the end of your faith, even the salvation of your souls" (1 Peter 1:7-9).*

GOD is love, and the story HE has written out for your life, is pure, and unchanged love. The horror comes in when you leave HIS perfect will to write your own story. Satan always presents this wonderful "you can have" story to our imaginations, and many times; we bite it without hesitation. GOD says that we can have anything we ask or think, but we have to believe for it. We know that sin will keep us from it, so we know that we need to walk that straight and narrow road to get to it. There aren't too many people on this road, so we get lonely, and we want the companionship of friends and lovers. Satan comes along and offers us everything that GOD has offered us, and he presents this blueprint of us having fun right now. According to his script, we could sin and still get to this blessed place. When we look on his road, it is broad and the majority of mankind is on it. Is this where the party's at? This road looks like a lot of fun and you reason with yourself that you can just tell people about the LORD while you are on it.

On this road are thieves, murderers, blasphemers, adulterers and all types of evil men and women. You can't trust anyone. Along the way, you see many fall dead, but you turn your head and keep on going because you can see the lights of change ahead. Not to mention, there are the ones who seem to have arrived at this wonderful place that Satan has offered you and this is motivating you to keep pressing forward. Then it happens. The doctor says that death has put you on its waiting list, but how can that be? Satan promised you long life and happiness, and it doesn't seem too much further ahead. How could GOD let this happen to you seeing that you have been telling people about JESUS all the while following the lead of sin?

You have to stay in GOD'S story; it is the only story written for your life that has a happy ending. It is a story written in love by Love! Satan's story for you is a short story, and it's full of drama, bad casting, low-budget episodes, and worst of all; the good guy always dies at the end.

It's your story. Tell it how you want to tell it, but know that in every story of our lives, GOD is the publisher and the editor. And once we're done telling the stories through our decisions, GOD will add HIS own already-declared Word to our stories. I'd rather HIM read a love story that reads like poetry and makes HIM smile than for HIM to read my life and weep because I chose to write a book about me being in sin. It's your story. How will it read?

CHRIST'S EDITS

We all had this wonderful idea of a life recorded in our mind's eye, and we did whatever we could to get there. You couldn't get to the celebrity that you had a crush on back in the day, so maybe you took his or her lookalike and you planned to marry them and have children with them. But, it didn't work because that celebrity went out of style and a new one hit the scene. As you grew older, you found yourself having friends whom you thought would be there for a lifetime, and boyfriends or girlfriends whom you thought would become your spouse one day. It didn't go that way, however. Instead, you have to come up with another friend, another mate, and then....come up with another plan for your imagination to feed off of. Again and again, you have seen your plans fall through the cracks, and life kept dealing you a script that you were unprepared to read. Nevertheless, you had to read it anyway.

We often imagine the story that we want to play out for our lives, but we often find our life's books being edited, the characters being changed, and the chapters ending in ways that we didn't see coming. Many times, we want to know why GOD removed our best friends from our lives, why HE didn't let us marry the person we wanted to marry, why HE didn't give us the job that we wanted to have. The answer is simple; your story did not match HIS story for you. You tried to recruit characters for the script without HIS approval, and they didn't fit into HIS vision for your life. Now, that it has been explained, you should be able to move on; right? But, it's not that simple for you. HE'S GOD. Why doesn't HE just change the script to give you what you want? After all, you have promised to serve HIM in your new role. You have to understand that GOD has a plan for all of us, and when our plans do not coincide with HIS, something has to give. Why would you think that the Creator has to honor the creation's blueprint for how he or she wants to be molded? What if your car decided that it wanted to go in reverse while you had it in drive? After all, it made a decision, and it wants to live its life in reverse. Why wouldn't you just honor that? Why would you take it to a mechanic and try to get it fixed? It's not broken if it's making its own decisions, right? When that car decided to go in reverse, it altered its original design, and anyone who drove it would put themselves and anyone else on the road with them or in the car with them in imminent danger. You are the same way. You have a design, and your design is created to follow a certain plan. Sure, you want to go backwards when the LORD is calling you forward, but if HE allowed this, your life would be in danger and the people who are closest to you would be in danger. Not to mention, HE gives us all free will. The people who you want in your life have their own abilities to make decisions and GOD will never kidnap someone's will to force them to honor your plans for their life. Lastly, GOD knows what could and would happen if your plans were to be followed through. Yet, HE still allows us to go out and will ourselves into HIS will for us or will ourselves into Satan's will for us. Your plans are Satan's plans when they do not match GOD'S plans. Satan doesn't care how much you go to church or how long you fast if you are willing to disobey GOD.

GOD gives us the opportunity to choose to do right or do wrong, but HE still edits our lives after letting a few scenes play out so that we can see the characters whom we have allowed into our stories. Review how Israel wanted a king. They demanded that they be given a king, and this was not GOD'S original plan for them. HE wanted to be their King, but they wanted a man to rule over them, so GOD gave them Saul. Israel chose to change the story, and as a result; they paid greatly for it. David was anointed by GOD to become king after Saul, but Saul wanted his son, Jonathan, to be king. So, Saul did everything in his power to kill David.

Let's see how this contrasts with your story. When you decide that you have a better script for your life than GOD has, you become irate and impatient with GOD. Often times, HE will let you have what you think you want. Let's say that it's that beautiful girl who's been passing by your house every day. GOD knows who she is and what she is. HE knows what dwells on the inside of her, and HE knows what her story entails, but you want her, and you have to have her, so you get her. GOD may have had a plan for you that involved greatness! Let's say, for example, that you were called to be a Bishop, own several lucrative businesses, and have five children. But, here you are with this character that you have chosen to replace the character that GOD had planned to serve as your wife, and this woman does not believe in your talents. Nope. She wants you to get out there and work two jobs! On top of that, she only wants two children, and when you talk about church, she's disgusted. Sure, she will go to church with you a few times, but her heart isn't there. Your heart, however, has been yearning for the LORD. You love HIM with such a great intensity, but your idea of a revised wife loves money and looking like a movie star. Because of her, you don't have time for church anymore! Chop-chop; you need to hurry up and get to that second job so that you can get her that car she's been whining about. You already know what's going to happen if you don't maintain her hollowness. She'll be trading you in for a newer model. Then, you find yourself crying out to GOD. Why did HE allow this great tragedy to become your life? You did that! You chose to alter the script, and you chose a bad cast. The LORD kept editing your plans, but you kept complaining and begging to have things your way, and GOD let you see how your way would play out on life's stage.

As we mature in HIS WORD, we begin to understand just why HE edited our lives the way that HE did. There were times when the devil planned to kill you in your sin, but GOD edited the ending and gave you a chance for a new beginning. That car narrowly misses you, and you'll immediately thank HIM aloud as you navigate your way to your destination because HE spared your life. Why are you not thanking HIM for editing the people out of your life that HE fired from your story? He was protecting you still, but it's hard to see that because you didn't know how the story would end, but HE did.

CHRIST will only have to edit your story when you change the original script. GOD has a plan for you, and if you would trust HIM and ask HIM to let HIS will be done in your life; you will find that HIS plans are far greater than your own. When you meet a person who you think has the potential to be your husband or wife, pray about them. Don't pursue them as the GOD-ordained spouse until GOD has confirmed that they are who HE has chosen for you. Otherwise, to marry a person who GOD did not choose for you would require a change in your story, and this change is NEVER for the best. Too many people's stories have ended in the graveyard because they wanted what they wanted, when they wanted it. When you meet a person who you think is going to be a great friend to you, pray about them. Don't sit there and thank the LORD for sending you your new best friend because this person may be someone who's passing through your life. They are trying to form their own stories and anytime two people try to merge their stories, someone's story has to be trashed. You should know from Jonah that living outside of purpose could cost you your life. Anytime you choose to live outside of your design; you will be swallowed up by something.

Take your plans to GOD and ask HIM to remove what you want and replace it with what HE wants. HE said that HE would give you the desires of your heart. Now, that doesn't mean you should keep that boyfriend or girlfriend that your heart desires, but what that does mean is that GOD knows what it is about that person who you are in love with. The husband or wife whom HE anoints and appoints for you will carry a greater height, greater anointing and greater love for you than that person you wanted to take down the aisle. If you wait on the LORD, when you look back and see the people who you wanted to cast with you; you will understand why HE said "no." You will thank HIM for every "no" that HE has ever uttered because HIS "no" is HIS protection!

You've got a story to tell. HE has already written your story. It is your choice which story you choose to be a character in, but know that HIS desires for you are far better than your desires for yourself. Trust HIM.

ADDING AND DELETING CHAPTERS

Have you ever read a book and got to a chapter or a sentence that just did not make sense? It looked liked the author added it to the wrong book? You were following along well, until this chapter or sentence threw your off a bit.

Life works the same way, believe it or not. In our lives, we tend to add chapters, delete chapters, and place the wrong punctuation in places, and this changes the meaning of each sentence that we are serving.

Adding Chapters
Oftentimes, we find ourselves in situations where a life-changing decision is upon us. There are two or more roads that fork off from our paths, and we have to decide whether or not to keep going on the road that we'd been on or to take another path. Now, most people would say they would continue on because they'd come too far to start over anywhere else, but in truth, the majority of believers take off in another direction. That's because when we are at these cross-roads, we reminisce on what we have met along the road that we'd been on, and we often find that we have not accomplished all that we set out to accomplish. Then again, there are the times we may feel that we've taken everything that route had to offer. A believer believes something; that's why he or she is called a believer. We like to think of that word in the context of believing in GOD,

but that word is inclusive. A believer believes something, whether it is the truth or a lie. Now, as believers in CHRIST JESUS, we believe HE is the Son of GOD, and HE died for our sins. We believe that HE was crucified, and HE was resurrected on the third day. But, is that all we believe? No. Sometimes, we believe our situations have more power than they really have and this causes us to add chapters to our stories that don't make sense.

Then, there are the optional ways of handling situations that the enemy presents to us. He tells us that these "ideas" can and will put an end to the situation immediately. He tells you to trust in your own devices. We've all fallen into this trap before, only to find ourselves in situations that are worse than the first ones. There are times when we used our own devices, and it looked like they worked. That's when we started trusting in ourselves. The problem is that what we send out has to come back to us. Our fixes are like bumpers duct-taped back on to the vehicle. Sure, it looks like it'll stay put until you push that gas pedal.

When adding chapters, we cause other chapters to emerge. These chapters are called trials, tribulations, and chastenings; and sometimes, we can cause our books to close entirely. You should always remain on the path that GOD has placed before you, even if you haven't seen much progress on it. In GOD'S will, you are constantly moving forward, but there are sentences where GOD has called you to see nothing and hear nothing so that you can learn to depend on HIM. You may not think you are making progress, and you are right because GOD is moving you forward! You can't do anything on your own, and anytime we try to work it out; we are actually going backwards.

Deleting Chapters
I was the queen of deleting chapters. If I did not like what a person was writing in my story, they were automatically removed from it. If I did not like a situation, I'd remove myself

from it. I saw the people who stayed in bad situations as weak. Why would someone tolerate pain when they could simply walk away? But, in truth, they were being buffed and polished, and I was the one that was weak. I was too afraid of the process.

When you and I were younger, we had to endure the wrongs that happened in our parent's houses because we had no place else to go. Even if we did, it often looked worse than where we were. Therefore, we endured the tears, the anger, the resentment and all that came with it while promising ourselves that our 18th birthdays would signify a change. We'd be old enough to go off on our own, and we wouldn't have to tolerate the hardships that came from our parents, siblings or any other relatives. We waited and waited and finally; our 18th birthdays arrived, but we weren't exactly financially stable enough to move. After having just finished high school, your options were to go to college or get a job. Either way, you wouldn't be able to afford rent, utilities and other living expenses. So, you may have gone to college or just started working, and you had to endure the family even more. It was a little easier because you were not at home as much and, by then, you probably had your own transportation so you could kidnap yourself from your parent's homes if things started getting chaotic. You stuck around another three years, and even at 21 years of age, you found that you could get a place, but you'd be struggling financially. You endured the process because you had to. You learned the importance of going to college, and the importance of staying busy. You learned that when you have too much time on your hands, you will always fight with the people around you. You couldn't delete this chapter because this chapter was put in place to help you grow up before you decided to go out on your own.

Now, that's not to get this mixed up with chapters that we added on our own. Some chapters have to be deleted because they were not headed by GOD. This was never a chapter HE placed in our books; therefore, to continue writing in them is sin and will prove to be deadly to our destinies. That friendship that you picked up along the way could be an example. Some days, you don't know if that person is your friend or foe, but the two of you have been going at one another for a long time now and reconciling over and over again. You think that this is healthy because you keep looking at the fact that you did reconcile and laugh about it, but what you don't see is the devil laughing at you. Anytime confusion is present, GOD is absent. We often look at the height of the "good times" and base our decisions on those while ignoring the depths of the "bad times."

Imagine this: You own a bank, and you have just hired an employee. He looked to be a promising employee, and he had some of the same visions for the bank that you have. After hiring him, you notice that he does weird things like try to go into the bank's vault with other employees, he's always looking nervous, and he comes to work an hour before his shift is to begin. Now, all of a sudden, a string of robberies seem to target your bank and your bank only. These robberies always take place when this employee is off work and there were a couple of times that the bank was robbed when he was at work, but he didn't seem nervous at all. You tell the police about your suspicions, but they don't have enough evidence to prove that he's behind the robberies, so after questioning him, they release him. The next day, he's back at work. Would you keep him there or go ahead and fire him?

Let's say, for instance, that you did fire him and the robberies suddenly stopped. Now, you are sure that it was him, but another problem arises; you miss how neat he used to keep the bank and his friendly demeanor. Even if he was robbing you blind, he was your star employee. So, you go back and rehire him again and the two of you talk. He assures you that he was not the one robbing your bank, but he believes that someone that doesn't like him was trying to frame him, so they made it look like he was the one. He goes on to give you all of these great stories, and the two of you reconnect.

Suddenly, the robberies start again; but this time, the bandit is determined to not be caught, so he forces the employees to the ground and promises to shoot anyone of them that looks at him. You're not ready to go back down this road, so after the robbery you fire the guy once again. Now, your bank isn't so organized anymore, and you miss this guy once again. What if he was innocent and the victim of some ignorant character who wanted to ruin his life? How could you play a role in this, knowing that he has a family to feed? So, you go back and rehire him again. As long as you continue to do this, that robber is going to become more brazen with his behavior and more dangerous.

This is the same thing that happens in friendships or relationships that were not authored by GOD. We always have excuses for the characters, which gives them more time to rob us of our destinies. Therefore, some chapters absolutely HAVE to be deleted if we want to walk into the next chapter GOD has in place for us, and if we don't, we go into another chapter that Satan has written for us.

You should only delete chapters that were not added by GOD!

<u>PUNCTUATING YOUR LIFE</u>

There is a popular adage that people use: "Don't place a comma where GOD has placed a period." That is so very true, but the truth is broader. We often place periods where GOD intended a comma to go. For example, many of us end our marriages when GOD intended for us to stay in them. Sometimes a period just makes sense. It makes sense mostly when our hearts are full of unanswered questions, hurts, and regrets. A period marks the end of a sentence, or in our cases, the end of a statement made in our lives. We can decide if we want to end the entire chapter there, or continue it with another sentence. A sentence marks a period of time in which a statement is being made. With our lives, we tend to make statements a little longer than we should have because human beings like to prove a point. We love being right, and we love when everyone sees that we are right. This is rooted in our own self-conceit, and that's why we are not supposed to argue the WORD of GOD with anyone. Arguments stem from pride, conceit and the desire to be the smartest of them all. When we share, for example, what GOD wants us to share, HE wants us to end it with a period so that HE could glorify HIS Name. All too often, we want to place a coma there and continue on and on about why we think we are worth listening to. This is especially true for women. We argue non-stop with our husbands, and we torture our children for hours on end when we are not happy with their decisions, whereas, all we were supposed to do is state the truth and leave it alone. People have to fall down before they learn the value of standing up.

There are seasons in our lives that were ordained by GOD for us to enter, but often, we don't know when or how to walk away from the season once GOD has ended it with a period. We don't like to hurt or offend people, even though we know our season is up in their lives, so we stick around trying to be that "friend" that sticks closer than a brother. Any chapter that you enter that was not written by GOD is authored by the devil, and every chapter that was closed by GOD can never be reopened. It doesn't matter if that chapter is full of GOD-fearing people and testimonies, if GOD has placed a closing mark behind it, you will have to go into sin to reopen it.

This gives Satan permission to attack you because Satan dwells in darkness, and every form of sin is darkness. When we are out of the will of GOD, we are in the will of Satan. There, he can serve you whatever he wishes to serve you, unless GOD says otherwise. When we stand in closed chapters, we are, in reality, saying that we want to continue the story. The problem is that GOD has made HIS closing statement involving that chapter. Any add-ons to the story did not come from GOD.

Think about those situations that started off as a huge blessing. You knew that GOD was in it, and you glorified HIM because of it. All of a sudden, those same people who you once blessed GOD for are attacking you. You might think, "Wait a minute. How can they be GOD-serving? How did those miracles proceed from them, and how could they turn around and do the will of Satan? What happened?" The story ended; that's what happened. You continued on with them because you saw what GOD did through them, so you began to revere the man and not the LORD.

Sure, you blessed GOD with your mouth, but your eyes were

focused on the man. You stuck around because you felt like this was a man or woman of GOD indeed! And they probably were, but when they entered another chapter with you, they entered a chapter not written by GOD. Satan wrote their scripts, and he wrote your scripts. Now, you're sitting there making a sequel to a story that GOD has ended. You were supposed to be in another chapter now. More often than ever, we go back to closed chapters and place question marks, comas and exclamation points where GOD has placed a period because we like or dislike how the chapter ended. People often find themselves in heart-gripping pain because they have moved beyond the period (.).

Then, there are the questions. Question marks tend to haunt women, especially. If something touches us in the wrong way, we like to catch the messenger or person who delivered that mess to us and interrogate him. We want to know "why" they are there, "when" did they get the chance to betray us, "who" sent them, and "how" could they do these things to us after we've been so good to them. We like to compare what we would have done to what someone actually did, and if it does not match up, we prosecute them in our hearts using our own self enacted laws. We put our hands in divinity when we try to imagine what's going to happen tomorrow, and we try to stop it today using our own devices. Satan likes to present the current situation to us, show us the math and then show us how he says our future will look if we don't do something about it immediately. He then presents us with alternatives to GOD'S way. He reminds us of the sins we've committed and then says to us that GOD isn't listening to us because of these sins. This entices us to take alternate paths outside of GOD looking for a solution. No matter what answer you come up with, you will be wrong if GOD never gave you the test to take in the first place. The right thing to do is stay in HIS will.

When you are haunted by questions, it is better to ask GOD for answers and turn to the Bible. Often, the answer is already in the Bible, but we like to live life without reading its manual and then call the manufacturer when we begin to seek break-downs. Turning to man for answers will always bring about more pain and more questions because man doesn't have the answer for himself.

If a man married a promiscuous woman, and she cheated on him, why would he ask her the reason for her infidelity, seeing that she doesn't understand it herself? She's just promiscuous, but often, a man will drive himself into a murderous rage trying to bring answers out of a person who has questions. She first needs to ask the LORD why she is like that before she can answer that man.

The exclamation points stand for the points of authority in our lives. Ending stories with an exclamation point reflects to the reader that something in this story has struck a nerve in you. You can react against the enemy, speaking in authority and closing chapters and doors that are demonic in nature. Then again, sometimes people scream at their lessons because they don't understand that GOD is allowing them to go through these lessons to glorify HIS Name. We have to know when to speak in authority and who is the author of our stories.

Anytime, you continue a sentence that should have been ended; you will change the meaning or the intended message of that sentence. Let GOD speak through you in every way. HE knows when a chapter ends and when the next chapter begins. Never go back into the previous chapter to add your own marks; you'll be wrong every time. Instead, remember to let GOD be GOD and let HIM punctuate your life. If you don't, you're going to find your life full of never-ending sentences of heartache, emotionally charged exclamations and misplaced periods of time where you could have been in your blessing, but you chose to remain in your curse.

YOUR DIALOGUE

Your life's dialogue is your verbal or written communication between you and others. Your emotions set the stage for the punctuation that ends each statement. For example, when you're angry, it can be heard in your tone and through your choice of words. If we were to write them out, you'd see a bold exclamation point behind much of what you say. This would help us all to pay closer attention to how we communicate with others as well as show us who we need to stop communicating with.

Believe it or not, your dialog is one of the most important parts of your life's book. The words you choose will either call GOD'S blessings or GOD'S wrath to you. In addition, Proverbs 18:21 reads, *"Death and life are in the power of the tongue: and they that love it shall eat the fruit thereof."* Your mouth is a womb that is always delivering. You are either pushing out a blessing, a curse or just idle words; but either way, everything you speak; you give life to. You might not see what is being born of you, but whatever you lose will come to either free you or bind you. You will come across people who are always miserable and their words reflect not just how they feel, but where they are spiritually. Each word that proceeds from their dark heart binds them even more. When they complain, gossip or lie; it takes them into the wilderness, where they complain more, lie more and gossip more. They keep wrapping cords around themselves with their own tongues, and they are frustrated with GOD, frustrated with life and frustrated with happy people because misery thrives in their hearts.

If you jogged by them at the park, it would be better to pretend that you don't see them because if you ask that infamous "how are you doing" question, the answer will always be the same: *"(Sigh) I'm okay. Just tired, you know? I've been feeling down every since I lost my job three years ago. The doctor said that I may have to come back for more tests on Monday; he's already found like five things wrong with me and to top that off, Momma has been fighting the nursing home staff again. They are talking about expelling her from that nursing home and I don't know where she's going to go if they do. My oldest son is running me crazy because he got his girlfriend pregnant and my daughter shuts herself in her room all day. I think it's because her stupid daddy left us 14 years ago and she's still feeling it. I need to get my medication, but I don't know where I'm going to get the money from and nobody in the family is trying to help me out. I helped Lucy out when she needed it, but every time I ask her for a dollar, she says she doesn't have it. One doctor says that I suffer from clinical depression and he said that I'm not supposed to be under a lot of stress, but how can I not be with all this going on? My car has been making strange sounds and I got ingrown toenails. Then my pet hamster got loose yesterday and my daughter accidentally sucked him up in the vacuum. So, now we got to bury him and I have to stop by the store and spend my last dollar buying her a condolence card. (Sigh) But, I'll make it. How are you?"*

People really do this! Their every word is a cord that binds them to something else, and you have to watch your dialogue with them to keep from binding yourself with your own words. When we come in contact with negative people, we feel the need to talk negatively so we can show that we can relate to them. The problem is that you should not want to relate to this character.

You should also monitor your communications with others. Pay attention to the information that is shared between you and the people who you communicate with. Your dialogue will often show you whether GOD is in your midst or not. When the conversations are full of flesh, GOD is not there. You may have some friendships that start off great; the two of you talk about GOD, edify one another and share testimonies. After a while, there is nothing else to share except the activities of the day. This is when you begin to share minute details of your day and how you felt at certain times in the day because the two of you have spent one another. Your conversation starts sounding like, "I was chewing a piece of chicken today, and I had a revelation. This chicken died so I can eat. Isn't that something?"

Idle dialogues are an indication that the two of you are spending too much time sifting one another when you need to dedicate that time to GOD and Kingdom work. If your communication isn't birthing something; it's killing something, even if it's just time.

Be mindful of what you say and what is said to you. Often, we carry on communications with people who unintentionally speak word curses over us. I remember dealing with a young woman whom the LORD had used me to minister to, but I had overstayed my season. She began to call me every day, several times a day just to discuss any and everything about her day. At first, when it was ministry, it was fine; I just didn't answer the phone when I was busy. I felt like it would die down eventually. After she'd come out of her trial, we were simply just "shooting the breeze" and whenever I would say something that was funny, she'd laugh and scream, "Girl, you are so stupid!" I knew what she meant by that because it is now used as an expression to say that you are funny, nevertheless, the word has already been defined, and its true definition won't change. I kept feeling convicted and feeling the LORD urge me to tell her to stop doing this because she was speaking word curses over me.

At first, I said nothing. I would just rebuke her words silently and keep talking. One day, I was sitting at the computer, trying to work, and I couldn't think of anything. I had been enduring periods of time where I felt like I couldn't work, write or think. I felt stupid. I would have to pray this off me, and the LORD brought her words back to my remembrance, "Girl; you are so stupid!" So, I waited for the next time that she said it, and I told her that we were going to have to find her some brand new words.

Eventually, I had to separate myself from her because GOD was no longer in the midst of our communications. The point here is: Your dialogue will set your character up for failure if it is not in the realm of faith. Most of us are still re-learning how to speak in a manner that doesn't leave a curse behind, but in the meantime, we have to be careful of our dialogues. Anytime you find your communications becoming less about GOD and more about you; you're spending too much time in idle flesh. If you're talkative and simply like to talk, this may be an indication that you have an anointing to speak or write. Why not translate what you want to say into a book, play or speech? Writing serves as a good outlet, and we are more careful about what we write than we are about what we say. It's okay to have a laugh and talk about life, but do the math and average out how much time you spend idly speaking every day. If you spend three hours just chatting every day, that's time that you could have used to actually complete something. It's one thing to start, but it's a blessing to finish. Again, if your communication is not birthing something; it's killing something.

Don't loan your ears to gossip, complaining or anything that hinders, because just as it binds the speaker, it comes with its cords to wrap you up as well. An unguarded heart is like a city without walls and everything that is spoken into your hearing is auditioning for a part in your heart. Eventually, it'll get a role, and you'll have to go through deliverance right alongside your friend. If your dialogue isn't one that GOD would be a part of; it's time to correct yourself, protect yourself and reject yourself.

Correct Yourself: This is when you acknowledge that you are wrong and GOD is right. Repent and get back in HIS will before your tongue births something that you can't hold.

Protect Yourself: Love people enough to tell them the truth. Stop worrying about offending them. Would you prefer to offend the LORD? I hope not. Don't let anyone speak anything that you don't want to come true in your life. If they call you crazy, and you don't want to be crazy, protect yourself by correcting them. If they get angry with you, it's time to part ways. No one should ever be upset because you asked them to stop cursing you.

Reject Yourself: Yeah, you're human and sometimes you don't feel like working, ministering or doing anything, but talking. You had this super eventful day, and you can't wait to share the "going ins" and "coming outs" of your day with your best friend. Ask yourself this: What is he or she going to do with that information? Will it bless me? Will it bless them? Will it bless anyone? What did you learn from that situation? If the LORD gave you a message, why not write it so it can bless a nation? Even if it's not a book, it can be an article that you post to your website, another website or local newspaper. Don't give in to yourself, give in to GOD'S will.

Don't just look at the whole book of your life right now, think about how your today is reading to GOD. Often, we write the wrong things Monday through Saturday and think that we can make up for it on Sunday. How did your today read to GOD? What have you done today that benefits the Kingdom of GOD? If your life was only 24 hours long, what inheritance would you have left for your children today? If your life was only a week long, what inheritance would you have left for your children's children? It doesn't have to be monetary; sometimes the greatest gift that you can leave is wisdom. That's how much you need to dedicate your time to publishing a great day for the LORD to read. If you knew you had only a week; you'd probably write books, share testimonies and bless GOD, but we can't assume how much time there is left. We can only live each day as if it were our last.

Your dialogues do affect you, your children, your health, your finances, your marriage and your life as a whole. The tongue sets loose some wicked things that can only be slain with the WORD of GOD. If you must dialogue often, do it with GOD. HE'D love to hear from you outside of the religiousness of nightly prayers and Sunday prayers. And if you've got friends calling you out of your name, you will eventually become what they have spoken because you have given them permission to speak into your life. I can almost guarantee you that if you stop them from speaking evil to and of you, they will cut you off. Why? James 4:7 says it best, ***"Submit yourselves therefore, to God. Resist the devil, and he will flee from you."*** Sometimes folks come to curse you, and because you let them, they call you friend.

CO- AUTHORS

Many of you don't like how your story is reading because you've got the wrong co-authors writing in your life. Believe it or not, they will answer for their sins, but you will answer for the sin of allowing them to scribble ignorance throughout your story. The Bible tells us that evil communication ruins useful habits. Evil communication does not mean to communicate with evil people. You have to share the WORD of GOD with the unsaved; that we know. Evil communication is basically not guarding your heart and allowing evil to be poured into it. For example, let's say that you were ministering to a young woman who was in fornication. You are telling her that fornication is wrong, and you are sharing the gospel of CHRIST JESUS with her, and she is receiving what you are saying. This is not evil communication because what you are pouring out glorifies the LORD, and she wants to be poured into. Let's take that communication in another direction. Let's say that this woman is refuting what you are saying and telling you why she thinks you're wrong. To communicate further on the issue is sin because she has basically told you that she wants to continue in her sin. Or let's say that your friend is in fornication, and you are telling her that fornication is wrong, yet you listen to her tell you how her "special friend" came over and how the act of sex started. You should never allow someone to pour out their sin into your ears because it makes its way into your heart and takes a seat.

Pay attention to everyone who is in your life and ask yourself this question. As co-authors in your story, what are they writing on your life? Truthfully, you don't have to wait for the story to end with some people. You already know what they are going to write on your life, or if you don't know exactly what they are going to record, you do know that it won't be good. But, oftentimes, we continue with them anyway, hoping that their story will change, and they will write good things on the tablets of our hearts. As time goes on, as a co-author, they keep changing the direction of your story, and you find yourself frustrated with them. If a person's story is not reading right to you, why would you give them a pen to write on your life? To minister to someone is to basically give them the idea for another chapter in their life. They can take what GOD says and apply it and start all over again, or they can choose to continue telling the story as they've been telling it. If they choose to sin as a co-author in their story, there is nothing that you can write in their life that will change their mind. Ministering, again, is sharing with the hungry; ministering is not badgering someone into doing the right thing. We have "will," and we are either willing to serve the LORD, or we are not willing to serve the LORD.

Review your story. Who has been writing good things in your life and who has been writing evil all over your life? I have met so many people who have friends and family members in close proximity of their hearts, and these people have been doing all manner of evils against them for years. Yet, they continue because they believe that longsuffering means to suffer long with someone. Longsuffering means to be patient, and patience does not mean to patiently wait on someone to finish you off. Patience is to trust in the LORD and wait on HIM to move, but while you are waiting for this change to take place, you have to stay in the will of GOD. The will of GOD is that you cut off all evil communications; yes, this includes friends, family, and clergy.

Your story is being written right now, as you read this book. Sometimes, the answers we have been seeking are in plain sight, but we continue looking for answers. Why is this? Because we don't like the answers we are getting, so we look for someone somewhere to tell us what we want to hear. The answer is....get those wicked people away from you! Take back the authorship of your life and give all rights to GOD!

Let's look at your best friend; she has been writing on your life for years. Let's say, for example, that she's been writing all kinds of craziness in your story. She has merged her story with your story and your story now reads like:

- I bought Tonia a new raincoat today. I spent all that I had, but she's worth it.
- Tonia called me and was angry because I didn't answer her call. I was asleep!
- I suspect that Tonia slept with my boyfriend.
- I drove Tonia to work today. I wish she understood that I do need gas money.
- I talked to Tonia about my suspicions, and she assured me that she could never do this to me.
- I bought Tonia some new shoes because her shoes were beat up. I only planned to spend $40, but she upset me when she went and chose a pair of shoes that cost $75, knowing that was all I had!
- Tonia is angry with me because I rebuked her about choosing the $75 shoes. Oh well, guess she'll get over it.
- Tonia defended me today when these two girls were arguing with me. I love her! She's such a great friend! Yes, we have our problems, but she's always behind me when I need her.
- I took Tonia out to eat today and we laughed all day about her college professor.
- I drove Tonia to work today. Did she not see my gas

needle on 'E'?

- Tonia got paid and gave me $10. She's even taking me out to eat. What a great friend!
- I took Tonia to church with me, and she went to the pulpit to have hands laid on her! It seems like all of my counseling is working!
- So, Tonia wants to go back to the club, even though I have explained to her that I don't go to clubs; I serve the LORD! She got angry, so now, I'm getting dressed.
- Tonia doesn't seem to care too much about my new boyfriend.
- Tonia is angry with me because I am continuing with my boyfriend, even though she says she saw him with another girl.
- My boyfriend and I got married! Yay! Tonia was the maid of honor, but I wish she'd been more thrilled about me getting married.
- Tonia is telling everyone that my husband is a cheater, even though he's not!
- Tonia tried to fight me today because she says I've been acting "strange." Dear Tonia, I was on my honeymoon; what do you want from me?!

Do you recognize a pattern here? The person who is telling this story is doing more for Tonia than Tonia is doing for her. Nevertheless, she is refueled every time Tonia does one good thing for her. She has given Tonia a pen and allowed her to co-author her life, and when we are co-authors, we tend to get mad at people for writing something we don't want in the books we are writing. Even though it's your life, the people you let in it will often get upset with you because you are not telling the story they want you to tell or the way that they want you to tell it. Maybe you married a man they did not approve of, or you choose a career that they wanted. Or maybe they wanted you to wait until they got married, and then you could get married, but you moved ahead of them, and now they are angry with you.

Your co-authors are going to write on your life; that's a given. But, it is your choice whether or not you allow them to do so. It is always better to pray and ask the LORD to remove the people HE does not want in your story. The characters have pens, but the co-authors write chapters, delete chapters and sometimes try to take credit for the whole book, if it reads the way they want it to read.

The people who are closest to you are your co-authors, and everyone else has a part in your story. But, if your story is reading in a different way than GOD wants it to read, you will find yourself in unnecessary trials, tribulations, and chastenings.

YOUR LOOK COVER

What is your "look cover?" Is it how you look? Your "look" cover is not the face that GOD has given you, but your look cover is what you do with that face. Think about a book cover. Almost every book has one. The design of the cover does make a big difference. Any seasoned author knows that their book cover's design is the expression of their book's face, and how that book is presented will make a difference in how it sells. That is, unless you are a mega celebrity and everyone knows your work; then you don't have to put any effort into how your book cover looks. For the guys, think about a beautiful woman. If you were single, and you saw this woman you were interested in, you'd want to approach her, but what if she was frowned up as if she wanted to kill someone? You probably wouldn't approach her because she looks unapproachable. Just like everyone, she has a face, but she designed it with a frown. Therefore, you don't want to get involved in her life since it seems that she is living in a bad drama.

Your "look cover," therefore, is the countenance of your face. Your face's expression will often tell others just what is going on in your heart and in your life. Only a dramatic person will audition to be a part of a drama-filled life.

People often mask what's going on in their hearts and in their lives by presenting a smile to the world. Have you ever met someone who seemed so care free that you just felt you had to know them? You start hanging out with them, only to find that their life is full of drama and pain. You visit them, and their husband is calling them all sorts of names. They are cursing, and their children have no respect for them, but when you saw them outside, they looked like they had it all together. That's because they know how to sell themselves. Even though their "look cover" said that they were a love novel, full of poems and beautiful music, you find out, once you opened up their lives, that they were an action film, riddled with knife wounds and loud music. When we run into characters like this, it is normal that we pull away because we don't want what's in their hearts to be written on their lives. After all, they've sprayed graffiti all over their lives and devalued themselves; now you want them nowhere near your heart. How could such an innocent-looking person be so full of turmoil? Realistically, we are asking the wrong question. The question should be, how could someone so full of turmoil pull off the feat of appearing and presenting themselves to be so peaceful and innocent?

As a publisher, I have found that some people will publish anything. Many people have some great books in them, and then there are some who simply don't want to understand that writing is just not for them, or at least in that season. They saw one of their best friends writing, and they couldn't stand the thought of being left behind. So, they broke out their computers and started writing a book about nothing. The book may start off talking about the power of a vacuum cleaner, and then before you've gotten to chapter two, you're in a whole new country on a whole new topic. Most people won't finish reading these books because as human beings, we hate being confused. Some readers end up frustrated because a little confusion sets us up for a lot of commotion. The author didn't bother hiring an editor or a proofreader. Instead, the author decided to publish the book and pray for rain. They did, however, make one wise move; they hired a professional designer to create the cover. Sometimes, they even hired someone to help them come up with a catchy name, and this is what got you. This book with this interesting cover, and this thought-provoking title was sitting online begging to be bought, and you bought it. Three pages later, you're ready to declare war on the author, and you've still got 276 more pages of confusing text to go.

Isn't this what people do? They present themselves beautifully, wrapping themselves in the best of clothes and decorating their faces with the best of makeup, but once you buy into their front; you end up wanting a refund. They knew what to do with their "look cover" and because of that, you were sold. Don't get mad at them because you've heard that old adage, "Everything that glitters ain't gold." These people are actually geniuses because they have managed to sell themselves to some of the biggest critics. Now, genius doesn't mean that they are wise; it simply means they have learned to beat man's system.

Should you do this? Should you decorate your face with a smile when your heart is weeping? No. I like to quote Matthew 5:37, which reads, *"But let your communication be, Yea, yea; Nay, nay: for whatsoever is more than these comes from evil."* This isn't just saying "yes" or "no," but it's basically telling us to be direct with one another. Don't go around trying to convince each other of something and don't present a false lead, but instead, just be upfront. Anything else is witchcraft. Use wisdom, of course. If you're going to a job interview, smile and answer the questions, but before you go to this interview, you should have dealt with the problem at hand so you wouldn't feel the need to put up a front. We should never sleep on our problems. *"Be ye angry, and sin not: let not the sun go down upon your wrath" (Ephesians 4:26).* If we learn to cast our burdens upon CHRIST, we could freely presently ourselves as we are; but we put on faces to cover up what's really going on in our lives and in our hearts.

Your "look cover" reads a message to GOD. It is not only graced by your name, but it has a subtitle. John Jamestown, for example, may be your name and title, but your subtitle may read, 'Bitter Old Man.' Remember, as the day turns itself like a page in the sky, you need to present yourself as a renewed and changed creature. Today you should be better and wiser than you were yesterday, and tomorrow you should be wiser than you are today. GOD'S mercies are renewed every day, and GOD told you to be transformed by the renewing of your mind. Renew means to make new again. In doing so, your "look cover" will represent the great content that is in your heart. Life presents us with countless opportunities to acquire wisdom, knowledge, and understanding; but every situation will have two hands. In life's left hand is bitterness and unforgiveness, and in life's right hand is the wisdom that the situation carried with it. It is your choice which hand you take from.

You can present yourself beautiful to man, but GOD is reading the content of your heart. If what is in your heart doesn't match your "look cover," you won't like how your story ends.

THE REAL STORY

You look in the mirror, and this character is staring back at you. You have seen this character through many stories, but you've never really gotten to know the man or woman behind the mask. How can one say that you don't know yourself? You'd think you knew yourself better than anyone; outside of GOD, but in truth; we often know more about others than we do about ourselves. We see the potential on others, but we find it difficult to see on ourselves. So, we just tell our stories, day by day until tomorrow comes and turns the page. Prayerfully, we've left yesterday in yesterday, and we are telling a different story today or a blessed continuation of yesterday's story.

Who are you? What is your story? The real story behind you started when you were in your mother's womb. GOD knew you then, and HE knows you now. HE called you forward for a purpose, and once you entered this earth; your clock began to wind down. Just like that play has to end, and that movie has to end; your story eventually has to end, but your legacy can live on.

One of the hardest things to accomplish is finding one's own identity. Everyone has an idea of whom or what they think you are, but GOD has hidden your identity in HIM, and it is only in HIM that you will find your true identity. We all have clues as to who we are, but our stories are like puzzles; the pieces slowly come together to form the whole picture. Of course, you'd like answers, but life is a mystery that is only solved when we find out that the problem is ourselves, and we learn to go to GOD for the solution.

GOD has a story for you, and your story is your purpose. When you tell it right, it comes together to glorify the name of the LORD, but Satan wants to pervert your story and use it to propel darkness forward. So far, your story may have been an awful one for you. All of the challenges and hardships you have faced can either change your story to one where the bad-guy wins, and you find comfort in being the loser, or you can take every bad thing that has ever happened to you to show the world what GOD has brought you through.

Your real story starts when you begin to identify who you really are in CHRIST. This is when you can identify key points from your past and see how they link up to your future. Even those situations where you were hurt the most, often times are like connect-the-dot games where who you are and what you are is identified when all of the dots come together. This is why you shouldn't spend too much time dwelling on your past and what someone has done to you. Sometimes, what you think they have done "to" you is actually what they have done "for" you. For example, I remember when I was deep in the world and had a boyfriend. A woman I worked with was going to travel to Louisiana for a school reunion, and she asked me to come. I was a young girl, still staying home with my mother and siblings, so this seemed like a weekend of freedom. Sure, this woman was about 20 years older than me, but what did I care? She'd said I could bring my boyfriend, as long as we told her family that we were husband and wife. I was so happy. I get to act grown! (Even though I was about 20 or 21 years old.) Anyhow, before the trip, I had a dream that I was driving down this road, and I was in the car alone. In this dream, it was a sunny day out, and for no apparent reason, I went off the road and crashed. The next day, at work, I told the woman who I was supposed to be traveling with about my dream, and she became angry with me. She said that I was "jinxing" the trip, but in truth, I wasn't. GOD had given me a vision to see what was going to happen, just not the exact way it would play out. Anyhow, we left out later that day, and I wasn't driving, like I was in the dream, but my guy friend and I rode in the back seat because we wanted to sit together. The trip wasn't going too good because the woman who had invited me was fussing about my dream and then about little things I said. I wasn't wearing a seat-belt because I was sitting in the middle of the backseat, leaning over the armrest trying to argue my case. I asked her to slow down because she was driving too fast, and this made her complain even more. She told me she was driving before I was a twinkle in my daddy's eye, and I started getting offended because she just wouldn't stop complaining. My boyfriend at that time started agreeing with her, saying that I did this with him all the time, complaining about how fast he was driving. I got upset with the both of them, and I slid over behind the driver's seat to get away from him and to get out of her view. I leaned my head into the back seat and fell asleep. A little later, I was awakened by the sounds of screeching tires and screaming. It was dark and raining, and the driver had slammed on brakes trying to avoid hitting a car that had suddenly stopped in front of her. We ended up hitting the car anyway and spinning into a ditch.

At first, all of that arguing and talking about me seemed like something they were doing "to" me, so I took offense, but their words against me made me slide behind her seat. The act of sliding behind her seat, more than likely saved my life. Had I been sitting in the middle like I previously was, I would have undoubtedly been thrown through the windshield because the impact totaled the car. Even the way I'd positioned my head in her seat was in a protective way. GOD had tried to warn me in a dream of an impending accident, but I couldn't resist the temptation to go and play house with someone. Needless to say, HE still protected me and allowed what I saw as an attack against me, to be HIS protective arms covering me.

There are many situations that have happened to you that you have perceived as "bad," but they were and are not situations that happened against you. They happened for you. You see, when your real story begins to come together, everything that came into your life will play a part in pushing you into GOD'S will. Even those things, people, and situations that drew you away from HIM will eventually cause you to run back to HIM, if you heed the warning that they give. All things confirm that GOD'S WORD is truth! That terrible man you couldn't do without will show you why GOD said to seek first the Kingdom of GOD and all its righteousness. That horrible woman you had to have will turn around and show you why you shouldn't have had her. She will confirm that it is better to dwell on the corner of a rooftop than with an angry and contentious woman. Those children you refuse to discipline will confirm that a spoiled child is the result of a spared rod. That STD will confirm that it is better to marry than to burn. That friend who has you in the headlock, ramming your head into your own car, will confirm that evil association ruins useful habits. All that debt will confirm that you should owe no man anything, but to love them.

Stop the vehicle and get out where you stand. Lie before the LORD and ask HIM who you are and what's your real story. Stop telling the story of someone else with your life. You can't have what is written for him to have. You can't be who she is called to be. You can't pencil yourself into a story and expect it to read the way you want it to read. You can only follow the route that GOD has laid out for you so that you can tell your real story. Hell was not created for man, but for Satan and his angels. Nevertheless, if you don't believe that JESUS is LORD, then you are in the same, penciling yourself in as one of hell's residents.

You have to refuse to tell the story the way you think it ought to read and to read from the story that GOD has prepared. HE has given you the will to go left, right, back, and forward and HE has predetermined how HE wants to bless you. Now, HE hasn't created a line-by-line script for you because HE wants you to exercise your will. HE has, however, created blessings that are reserved for the righteous, and the greatest of them all is to spend eternity with HIM.

It is not uncommon for people to morph into characters people expect them to be. This is when we begin to tell a story that is not true by living a life that is not ours. You have to be willing to cut people from your story when GOD says it is time for them to exit the stage. Having the wrong people around will always cause us to tell the wrong story to keep them around or to keep them satisfied. Your story has merged with the stories of the people around you, and you may be causing their story to be a little more interesting, but what are they doing to yours?

If your story has been reading all wrong, it's because you're telling the wrong story. In other words, you are lying, and you are living a lie. Get back to CHRIST and follow HIM so that you can see that any story written by HIM is written for HIM. Anything that is for HIM is for you!

Go back to your mirror and look at that character again. Now tell the person looking back at you that you are going to find out just who they really are. So many of you have pure greatness in you, but you haven't found this out because you have not searched the heart of GOD to find HIM out. In HIM is where our masks fall off. This is where your story will begin to make sense, and every chapter will lead to the next chapter in perfect sync.

A STORY OF UNFORGIVENESS

A lot of the chapters in our lives have not started yet because we are still pages away from today, hurting about something that happened 3,650 yesterdays ago. We can never follow through with five o'clock when four o'clock is still on our watches. In other words, you need to forgive somebody somewhere.

Living in the past will never disarm your future, but instead, it'll arm the future against you because you're not allowed into today wearing yesterday's uniform. That's why people who let unforgiveness reside in them often find themselves deathly ill. They have died in the today to go and live in yesterday and now; their bodies want to stand in agreement with their minds.

Unforgiveness doesn't just want to be a part of your story, but unforgiveness likes to narrate your story. It wants to determine how your story reads. Unforgiveness has an undeniable voice, and it tells the story in such a way that anyone reading it will know who is narrating it. Once unforgiveness has become a part of your story, it will always reassign the roles of each character in your life. Your pastor, husband, and children are now the villains, and your real enemies are now your heroes. You suddenly take on the role of GOD in your life and GOD, to you, becomes nothing more than a word that you say. Unforgiveness reassigns roles that guarantee that your story ends in hell!

A lot of people will proudly exclaim that they have forgiven their enemies, but read their stories and you will see the truth. The people who have hurt them are still a part of their stories, even though they are no longer a part of their lives. These people still have power to move them. When I was living in my small hometown, I would often run into people I had been enemies with or had fought with a decade or so ago. I would speak to them, thinking to myself how silly we were when we were young because I've never been one to hold a grudge. The sad thing is, I've had people roll their eyes or do something that displayed they hadn't forgiven me for a fight from years and years ago. It truly baffled me that all this time later, people are still holding onto issues from when they were teens. When you don't forgive someone, you literally hand them a remote control to your life. They may not be able to tell you what to say, but they can turn you off or turn you on whenever they feel the need.

Why would you let unforgiveness be a part of your story? Here's a better way to tell your story:

- Silly me! We fought a long time ago when I was young and dumb and trying to establish an identity that wasn't mine! Please forgive the character I am for what the actions of the character I was.
- Silly me! I dated you when I was young and dumb, but I discovered that you weren't for me when you walked away from me because _____ (insert reason here.) Weren't we silly back then? I hope you are a better man or woman now, but not for me, for GOD and eventually for the person who HE permits you to marry.
- Silly me! You were my closest friend and I adored you, but you betrayed me greatly. I saw the signs, but I chose to ignore them. Howbeit, I love you anyway and I pray for you every night, that you see how much GOD loves

you and that you return to HIM wholly. I love and forgive you. Say hi to the family for me!

- Silly me! As a parent, I would have expected more from you! You hurt me, ridiculed me, and did whatever you could to break me down, but you know what? I survived you! Today, you are innocent of those charges of which I once condemned you. I had no choice but to be your son or daughter then, but I can choose now what you are to me, and I choose to be the person who prays for you. I choose to keep my distance from you to protect myself from what you are, but I still love you and wish that you would simply denounce your evil ways and pronounce the Name of GOD. Nevertheless, I choose to be a better parent, learning from your mistakes so they don't have to become my mistakes. I love you much.

It's your story. You choose how it is going to read. In the end, it will be GOD who reads your story back to you, and you will wish you could go back and edit that story with a state sized eraser. If you could see what GOD sees, you would fire many of the characters you have hired in your story because you'd know they are on demonic assignments. You may even think that some of the people who came to bring you down were unsuccessful in their attempts, but in truth, they were successful if forgiveness has you in shackles. Sometimes, the devil will send people into your life to bring unforgiveness to you, and these characters will do obvious things like try to date your wife, but she's a good woman, so she turns him down and tells you. Now, you hate this man with all your heart, and you tell anyone that will listen how this man thought he could slither behind your back and lie with your wife, but it didn't work. What you don't know is...Satan knew she would say no. The whole scene wasn't set up under the ruse that she'd say "yes." It was set-up to bind the man of the house. This is how demons can come and loot your house. ***"Or else how can one enter into a strong man's house, and spoil his goods, except***

he first bind the strong man? And then he will spoil his house" (Matthew 12:29).

People often forget that Satan is crafty. They think they see him in the east winds, and they set up brigades to the east to protect themselves and their families, but he'll turn around and attack them from west. Your boss may have been horrible to you. You probably prayed, for example, that your boss is dealt with for making your job miserable. Let's say that the boss is fired, and now you're screaming, "Don't touch GOD'S anointed!" Sure, this is true, but when you see your old boss again, you are pointing him or her out to your friends and laughing about the series of events that left him or her jobless. You may have thought that this person was sent by Satan to cause you to lose your job, but GOD intervened, and the boss lost his or her job instead. The scenario that isn't considered, however, was that the boss was simply a pawn in Satan's attempt to attach unforgiveness to you. After his or her job was completed, he or she was let go. Maybe that same boss was planning to apologize to you or to try to reward you more because they have repented to GOD, but Satan didn't want them to get this far. They've gotten you to board yourself into unforgiveness and Satan doesn't want them knocking on your door and handing you an eviction notice. Instead, the more appropriate prayer would have been for GOD to cancel the assignment of the enemy against them and their families because the war is not of the flesh. It wasn't a war between you and your boss; that war was spiritual. (*See Ephesians 6*)

One of the easiest ways to fall into unforgiveness is to focus on people and what they do. When you care about what they think, they have power over you. When you care about what they do, they have power over you. When you care about how they do something, they have power over you. If you don't want people to have power over you, and if you don't want unforgiveness as a part of your story, you have to stay focused on HIM.

Remember, unforgiveness doesn't want just to be a part of your story, but it wants to tell the story of your life. Unforgiveness doesn't just plan to be a chapter in your book; it plans to be the editor, publisher, and promoter of your life. People never betray one another; we only betray ourselves when we believe man's voice over GOD'S. Any man or woman can say whatever they want to say, but if you would dare to tune into GOD'S voice and listen to what they are really living, you won't wrestle with forgiving them. The hands come together to assume the praying position. When you learn to pray and ask the LORD to expose the tares in your life; HE does. That's when another prayer comes out. You then ask the LORD to remove the tares from your life, and HE does. That's when another prayer comes out. You then ask the LORD to keep all tares from you and to give you the wisdom to know the difference between a tare and a wheat, and HE does. That's when another prayer comes out. Because you have discovered that the people who you truly loved were tares, you now want to know why they came into your life and how they got in. HE answers, and that's when another question forms and another reason to pray is established. What you are doing is opening up a line of communication between you and the LORD.

When you don't forgive the people who have hurt you, you forfeit GOD'S "yea" and "amen" for your life. These promises are reserved for HIS sons and daughters. You can't have a bitter heart without it destroying your story.
You are writing the book right now. You can end the chapter on unforgiveness right now. Someone once said to me that forgiveness is a process, and this is not true. To forgive is a choice we make to proclaim the innocence of another person and to no longer hold them accountable for what they have done to us. Unforgiveness isn't an issue of someone wronging you; it is an issue of how you feel about them after they have

wronged you. If every time you see someone, you think about what wrong they've done to you, you need to go before the Throne of GOD and ask to be delivered from this cancer of the heart. People do repent and maybe they have repented for what they did. You can't stay in yesterday trying to hold their noses in the mess they've made in your heart. Instead love them all over again today as if they've never done you wrong, but keep the wisdom from the experience and know that they are not allowed within reach of your heart unless GOD says otherwise. GOD'S mercies started all over again for you today; therefore, your love has to renew as well.

Look at it this way and you should be okay:
Silly me! I hated you once, but I'll love you twice and even till the end of time. Even though I loved you here, I now love you there. Stay over there and I'll pray that my role in your life (and vice versa) is fulfilled in a way that glorifies GOD. No more silliness for me. I know that you had not paid the price to be in my heart, so you couldn't know the value of the space you were in. That's why you didn't take care of it, and it's not your fault.
Silly me! I put you in danger when I let you in there because I am GOD'S anointed, and as such, I am protected. Thank GOD that HE spared your life after you'd laid your hands on me or laid your mouth on me time and time again. It wasn't your fault; it was mine for letting you in when GOD told me to keep the doors of my heart guarded. If I leave a three-year-old in a running vehicle, I can't get mad at him for trying to drive it and crashing it into a tree. Instead, I need to be held accountable for placing him in harm's way. Silly me! But because I'm wiser now, I have taken back the keys to my heart, and you are no longer allowed in the driver's seat or anywhere near my heart. I have, however, asked the LORD to use me in your life in any way that HE sees fit, if this was and is HIS plan for me. I want to bless you, and I'm sorry for giving you a role that GOD hadn't given you, and then getting mad at you when you couldn't act it

out to perfection. I love you, and for what I've done to you, I ask that you forgive me because in truth, I'm the one who needs to be forgiven. I did you wrong because I gave you something that was too heavy for you to hold, and when you dropped it, I had the nerves to get upset with you. Can you forgive me?

DRAMA SCENES

A book is usually at its best when you enter the drama portion of it. Movies and plays are the same, but when it's our life, drama scenes aren't so entertaining.

Where does all the drama come from? Friction arises when two forces oppose one another. It is the result of two things traveling past one another in opposing directions. Now, you may meet some people who will proudly tell you that friction is healthy for you. A good debate stirs the soul, right? Wrong.

There are two forces in this world: the kingdom of darkness and the Kingdom of GOD. When two forces are opposing one another, there isn't a sharpening taking place. Instead, the strength of both opposing forces is being tested. Think about a sword battle. Hitting two swords together does not sharpen the swords, it dulls or destroys them. When a sword is being sharpened on a wooden sharpener, only the sword moves, but the sharpening tool stays still. When using an electric machine to sharpen a sword, the machine turns its wheels consistently and the foundation of the machine stays still, but the sword is moved back and forward until it is sharpened. If two metal wheels were spinning in opposite directions, neither one would be sharpened; but instead, they'd grind one another down to nothing, causing friction along the way.

You are built the same way. The WORD of GOD is the Sword of GOD, and only the Sword should be moving in your life. Your job is to move the Sword by opening your mouth, but trust GOD enough to be still and use HIS WORD as your foundation. ***"Be still, and know that I am God: I will be exalted among the heathen, I will be exalted in the earth" (Psalm 46:10).*** HE will sharpen you because the Sword of GOD is within you. When you choose, however, to turn your flesh's wheels against opposing forces, you will cause friction and this will only grind your faith down to nothing. You can't fight a spirit with the flesh. When there is opposition, there is the operation of two or more forces that are opposing one another. Opposition is basically the opposite of a position or the opposing of a position. GOD'S position is firm and obedience is your position of strength, nevertheless, anything or anyone who opposes your position is your opposition. And in truth, this opposition isn't really against you; it is against the force that is in operation in you. ***"For though we walk in the flesh, we do not war after the flesh: For the weapons of our warfare are not carnal, but mighty through God to the pulling down of strong holds...." (2 Corinthians 10:3-4)***

Some people love drama. Almost every family has this character in it, and if you don't know who they are, you might be that character. A dramatic person tends to always be in opposition to something. You say you want to have a family reunion in May, and they want to do it in June. You want to bring your husband on the family cruise, and they want to make it a girls-only cruise. You want the bridesmaids to wear purple gowns at your wedding, and they think purple is too tacky, so they try to insert their own wedding ideas into yours.

There are also dramatic friends who seem to always be mad at someone for doing something in a way they don't agree with. There are the dramatic boyfriends or girlfriends who always seem to disagree with your way of thinking.

Therefore, drama is the result of two people trying to force their views upon one another, but opposition is the result of two forces opposing one another. Drama is the manifestation of opposition or the evidence of friction.

What about your story? Is it one that is full of drama and friction? Did you know that when you and another person are constantly opposing one another, both of you are wrong? Trying to force someone to see it your way or even trying to force them to understand what the Bible says comes from witchcraft. Anyone who attempts to hijack the way someone thinks is operating in witchcraft. You may say, "No; I'm just trying to get my children to understand that the WORD of GOD is true, but they don't like to listen. So, I'm going to keep telling them over and over again until they finally understand." This is witchcraft in operation. *"So then neither is he that plants anything, neither he that waters; but God that gives the increase" (1 Corinthians 3:7).*

You lay the seeds, and GOD will water those seeds. GOD will often use you to water those seeds by being a tool of sharpening, but there is no power in your flesh to force a seed to yield its harvest. You can only uproot a seed or plant a seed, but when you constantly stir the ground, that seed doesn't get the chance to mature. It will usually die before it could yield its fruit because you are digging it up and planting it all over the place. You can't trust in your own devices, for JEHOVAH is GOD alone, and HE will give the increase.

Drama always opens its mouth when pride is on the scene. People don't like to be wrong because a lot of people are trying to earn the right to be right. That is, they want others to see them as always right so that they can secure a dominating position in these people's lives. For example, that mother who can never accept when she is wrong because she believes that in doing so, her children will not need her anymore. This is a way of thinking that always invites drama to the family picnics.

Unlike action movies, dramas in life don't always finish with a happy ending, since both people are in sin. It takes one person to contend, but two people to make it a drama. Your wife, for example, could come home and contend with you about how you've been acting the last few weeks. She feels like you've been distant and unappreciative, so she handles it by screaming and crying. Yes, she is reading from the wrong script, but that doesn't mean that you have to take on the role of an even more evil character. If you continue to write the story the way that GOD wants you to write it, you could disable whatever demonic force may be in operation against her. Her actions show that she is contending, but your actions will determine how that scene unfolds. Talking to her and being apologetic is the move of a wise and strong man. This scene could become a drama should you decide to be a hero and rescue yourself from her war of words.

Other than the spouse, there should be no character in your story who keeps on bringing the drama into it. I don't care if it's your mother, father, sister or brother; drama is opposition. Opposition makes life harder because as we try to move forward, a force is opposing our movements. Sadly enough, so many people have welcomed opposition into their homes and into their lives. What I found was that anytime someone brought drama to me, if I would stay humble, forgive them, but let them go, I would always stay in elevation. Why is that? I recognized the opposition, and I changed my position in their lives. Now, if you are doing wrong and someone opposes it, they are simply correcting (sharpening) you and this is an act of love, but opinions are oppositions that should be always delivered in meekness, with no expectation of acceptance.

The less drama around you, the more blessings will surround you. Sure, when your heart hurts or your pride has been wounded; you may feel some kind of way, and you want to redeem yourself, but you have to remember that vengeance belongs to the LORD. Humble yourself and do it quickly. It is always better to humble yourself before GOD than to be humbled by GOD. Let people be wrong. You don't have to accept their way of thinking if you know it is wrong. They have the right to be wrong, and if their wrongs don't affect you directly, then why are you fighting with them?

The best parts of our stories aren't the drama-filled chapters, but the chapters of peace are the ones that read the best before the LORD. And when drama finds its way to you, be still and know that HE is GOD. Don't spin your wheels in drama; but let the WORD in you sharpen you. Friction always causes heat, but let people be heated. Just pray for them from a distance. Remember this: Anytime you walk with drama; you oppose GOD, and this is not where you want to be, since anyone in opposition to HIM has already been defeated.

<u>BAD CASTING</u>

I looked around one day and saw that I was surrounded on every side by sinners who loved their sin. I was also in love with sin, so even though I was conscious about it, I kept them around a little while longer because I could relate to them. As my relationship with the LORD developed, I found that more and more of these characters were exiting the stage in my life. Soon, there was no one left but me, in front of an audience of family members who were accustomed to seeing the dead girl. They didn't want to see or know the changed woman; they'd come to see the evil and lost soul whom they believed was destined for a very dramatic and entertaining finish. But, I cried out to the LORD because I didn't want to continue in my sin, and I didn't know how to stop sinning. I knew it was wrong, and I knew what sin would eventually do to me, so I made up my mind to follow CHRIST and that is when something amazing began to happen. That familiar audience, one by one, began to exit the stage in my life because they didn't like my show anymore. Instead, many would tell others how horrible my show had become. How could old sinful Tiffany now all of a sudden think she was saved? I wasn't hurt about it anymore because I had become used to transition, and I knew that in transition, people had no choice but to leave. That show had ended, and I was preparing for my next show. For a long time, the audience was empty. At first, I found myself crying because there was no one around me I could relate to. The people from my sinful past wanted to exhume the dead me, so I elected to stay away from them, and the people I wanted to be around who were from the church, didn't want me in their midst because they didn't believe that I could be changed. I started to get angry with mankind as a whole, but then the LORD revealed something amazing to me. HE had called me to be alone so that HE could change my heart and prepare me for the next show. People were just distractions, so even if they wanted to be around me, they couldn't.

As HE changed me more and more, I began to understand why FATHER wouldn't let me near some of the folks I thought were righteous. My heart desired to serve HIM wholly. I'd done time in sin before, and I knew what was there, but I wanted to explore the heart of GOD. While I was trying to recruit new cast members into my life, the LORD was keeping me from my habit of having a bad cast in my story.

Is this your story? When the cast is bad, the show is bad. It is common for us to put people in roles that they are not skilled or anointed to have. We give our greatest enemy the role of the best friend; we give a loose and wandering soul the role as our adviser; we give a dead man the role of speaking life into our destinies; we ask unfaithful people to play faithful, and so on. It is funny when you think about it. And when the curtains go up, and the cast is failing; we want to cry out to the LORD, "Why did you let these people in my life?" HE simply allowed you to let those people in your life, and HE allowed you the flexibility to put these people in place so that you would know that you can never take HIS role as GOD.

Think about a puzzle. Let's say that your child is whining because you won't let him put the puzzle together like he wants to, so you decide to just let him, and he gets it all wrong. He's placed an eye where the leg should go and an ear as the belly button. After, he's forced these pieces together and distorted them, he looks at you and cries, "Why didn't you tell me that I was doing it all wrong?!" Now, if you're into corporal punishment, you'd probably spank him, and if you're not into corporal punishment, you'd probably engage in a verbal battle with him. Just like he has to be punished for verbally assaulting you when his own efforts fail, you have to be punished for verbally assaulting GOD when your efforts fail. We love to try to put the puzzle together ourselves when GOD has warned us that we can't do it without HIM. HE has to be the one to show us the big picture. GOD will let you move when you think you're strong enough or wise enough to put life's puzzle together, but once you've placed an enemy in the place of a friend, the wrong man or woman in the place of a spouse and a lie in the place of the truth; the right thing to do isn't to whine, but to repent.

But you're giving out roles anyway, and you hope that each character will act his part the way your imagination played it out for you. Anytime you decide to write and act out your own story; you decide to forfeit GOD'S plan for your life. An evil cast will never lead you to a standing ovation with GOD. No man or woman is so important that they are worth going to hell for or even having a hell-filled life on earth for.

Your cast will determine how your show plays, and the cast will always determine who is in your audience. Good people like good shows and bad people avoid good shows. Try to drag a van full of fornicators into a show that teaches that fornication is wrong, and you'd probably get whacked before you park that van. But, try to drive a van full of fornicators to a show about people doing what they are doing, and they'll give you gas money.

Sometimes the LORD will empty out our audience so that HE can grow us up and give us the original script....the Bible! After you have read it and learned your role, then a new audience comes in to witness the power of GOD in you. The original audience came to witness you dying at the end. They would've come to your funeral as well, and watched you in your last role. They would've even gotten dramatic, crying and talking about how good of a person you were. The people who know the old you won't accept this new righteous and living you. That's why you have to exit their lives. You can't have dead folks around you and not expect them to stink.

Take a moment and review your life. Look at the cast of characters and ask yourself if this is how you want your story to end. With the right cast, the show will go on, but with the wrong cast...it's curtains for you!

<u>YOUR RATING</u>

As we mature in CHRIST, our ratings should have changed. We went from living innocent lives to lives full of sin, and then we went back to CHRIST. Ask yourself this: In this month alone; if someone had read my story, how would they rate it? Would it be rated G, PG, R or would my story be X rated? If the story of last week was a movie or a part in a play, how would it be rated? When we learn to see things like this, we begin to develop a view into how GOD sees us. The human mind often likes to believe that it is above and beyond correction, and we often believe that if we're not sinning today as bad as we sinned yesterday, that we are now doing enough. In truth, sin is sin and there is no minimum sin that is acceptable to GOD.

Pay attention to your life's story. Have your ratings improved or are they getting worse? Are they simply staying the same, meaning nothing has changed, but the time? This will let you know if you have grown. For example, you may have lived your life deep in the heart of sin. Your life, at one point, may have been X-rated because of promiscuity or premarital sex. Like many, you thought you had the answer to life's great mystery: how to find happiness in what you want to do, not what GOD wants from you. As you grew in CHRIST, you decided to stop doing a lot of the things that separated you from HIM. You stopped having premarital sex; you stopped fighting; you stopped hanging with the wrong crowd and so on. But, at that time, your heart was still being cleansed from all of the filth that had been deposited in it over the years. So, when someone made you mad, you cursed them out. People in transition like to say, "GOD ain't through with me yet...." This simply means that they aren't exactly rated Godly yet. Nevertheless, our ratings aren't determined by what we let slip out of us; our ratings are determined by what is in us.

I remember my own transition. I was loving the LORD, serving the LORD, and trying to live my life in a way that I felt was pleasing to the LORD. My husband would do something that I didn't like, and at first; I'd warn him. I'd tell him how it made me feel, and I would go on trying to be holy. Then, he would respond in the wrong way or do something that further angered me, and before I knew it, I was cursing and talking about divorce. My heart was in captivity, and I didn't realize it. My solution to a problem husband was to make him someone else's problem, not mine. So, I thought that divorce was the answer, but only because divorce is like sickle cell; it carries down the trait generation to generation and in many cases, the children of divorced parents welcome divorce as an alternative. The choice is to repair the marriage and work at it or take the easy way out, and the easy way out seemed less dramatic to me. My heart was dark, but I didn't want to accept that because I'd tried so hard to clean it up. During this time, the LORD let me go through some pretty hard trials by fire to reveal to me what was in the depths of my heart. When I would see these things (after I'd calmed down), I would pray against them, and slowly but surely, I was delivered. I had to change my rating before the LORD because I know that this life is not my own, and I had to learn to love my husband as a wife should love her husband.

What if GOD had a rating scale? What if HE said that anyone whose life is rated X, rated R, rated PG-13, and rated PG could not enter Heaven? What if HE sent a tape of your life to the

Motion Picture Association and asked them to rate it? What do you think your rating would be? Where do you think you would spend eternity? While waiting for your rating, would you go ahead and stand in the line for Heaven or would you be honest with yourself and stand in hell's line? Or would you stand in the middle, hoping that they missed those X-rated scenes? Do you realize that your life is on constant play before the eyes of the LORD? Don't you know that your life is being rated as Saved or Unsaved?   Sinner or Saint? Jew or Gentile? It's sad because even the people of Israel would watch HIM perform these undeniable miracles and watch HIM slay their enemies, but they still dabbled in their own lusts. They still played with idolatry, and they complained against HIM. In reading about their lives, you would find that they were a really stiff-necked people who believed in doing their own will and not the will of GOD. If their lives were played out in a movie, not like the ones that are out today, but the true acts that they performed before the eyes of the LORD, that movie would have no rating. It would simply be illegal to watch, and you'd probably have to buy it on the black market because it would be too heinous, too gruesome, too X-rated, and just evil.

Today, mankind is the same, if not worse. Everyone wants to do as they please and live their lives in a way that pleases themselves, but there are hardly a few left that are ready to throw selfish desires away to serve the LORD. Instead, people try to bargain with the LORD, and HE'S not signing that deal. People like to say, "Well, I'm not that evil. I only sleep with my boyfriend (or girlfriend), and I have a few beers from time to time, but there are people out there raping and killing folks every day. So, I hardly think that GOD would condemn me since I'm not hurting anyone." But, with GOD, there is only holiness or hell. There is no beautiful way to sin, and no one can dress sin up, put ribbons on it and call it cute. Sin is sin, and it is hideous in the eyes of the LORD. A killer is condemned already according to the WORD, just like fornicators are already condemned. A killer's hell won't be any hotter than the hell of an adulterer. This is something many purposely overlook because they don't want to hold themselves accountable for their own sins. Many think that by not holding themselves accountable or by closing their eyes to the WORD of GOD that they are automatically exempt from the law of GOD. When they go through punishments, they think that they are just chance encounters. *"The way of the wicked is as darkness: they know not at what they stumble" (Proverbs 4:19).* But, to hold their self accountable means to deal with the burden of guilt and that overwhelming realization that a change has to be made to become acceptable vessels for GOD. We get caught up in living life a certain way, and we want to continue living in that manner, but when change knocks at our door, we shut the door and cut off the lights because mankind loves his dark habitations. Therefore, many continue on living sinful lives, and they hope that Heaven's camcorder is too grainy to see their faces. This is simply denial because, in truth, GOD sees and knows all.

Again, ask yourself; how is my life rating nowadays? Could children be allowed to watch your life play on a screen or would they have to be forbidden from watching you? Now, if you're married, I understand that there are scenes that no one could watch; but I'm not talking about these scenes. I'm talking about your life as a whole. Could your children or your nieces and nephews watch you on your day-to-day or would they be prohibited from seeing you until they were 18 years old or older? *"And Jesus called a little child unto him, and set him in the midst of them, and said, verily I say unto you, Except ye be converted, and become as little children, ye shall not enter into the kingdom of heaven" (Matthew 18:2-3).*

To become as little children is to have the faith, innocence and the resilience of a child. Children often are not swayed by society's influence. They love one another without looking at the social status, financial status, color, religion, or creed of another child. Instead, children are innocent and they love just because. Their lives are full of innocent gestures, (when they haven't been corrupted by man), and they are always willing to learn.

Today, decide to change your rating and consciously pay attention to the activities of your day. If someone in your life changes your life's rating for the worse, it is time to get them out of your life. No man, friend, or foe is worth being separated from GOD. **Seriously**. Pretend your life's story is playing in a theater before thousands of four-year-old children. Who, in your life, could possibly change the rating, thus making it inappropriate for that audience? Is it your Aunt Rita who loves to drink herself into a stupor and curse everyone out? Why is she coming by your house or in your life? You simply introduce the WORD to Aunt Rita and let her decide if she chooses HIM or not, but to let her pass out drunk on your kitchen floor is error. To let her walk into the doors of your home, cursing and carrying on is sin. If the four-year-old children can't watch the movie, it is time to stop watching it and change the characters.

What about your spouse? What if they were the reason that a child could not view your life? Your spouse loves to curse and listen to music that is full of profanity. What could you do to change your life's rating? It's easy for me to write, but it won't be so easy to activate in you since you are accustomed to handling your spouse a certain way. If you would dare to trust the LORD and serve the LORD, no matter what your spouse did, you will be the instrument that GOD uses to change the direction of your spouse's steps. That means, don't react profanely or violently if they do or say something that you believe came from Dumbville. Instead, try this and watch how you begin to infuriate and eventually run that devil off: When the spouse does something that makes you want to react in a negative way, give an opposite reaction than the one you want to give. For example, let's say your husband comes in late and starts to accuse you of running out the gas. You're ticked off because you know he's using this tactic to take the attention away from his coming in late. I can understand that your flesh wants to slap him with the door of a moving car. What you should do, however, is look at him and say, "I'm sorry, and I love you." Do you KNOW how much damage you do to a person when you react in a way that they didn't expect you to react in? When love comes on the scene, all the anger and stupidity, and the demons that dwell in anger and stupidity are exposed. With a spouse who is in sin, you simply need to obey GOD and refuse to let this spouse drag you into sin. In your obedience, either your spouse will eventually repent and come to the LORD, or your spouse will flee from you. ***"Submit yourselves therefore to God. Resist the devil, and he will flee from you" (James 4:7).*** If they choose to leave, being an unbeliever, you are to let them leave and know that GOD will bless you because you chose HIM over a man or a woman. ***"But if the unbelieving depart, let him depart. A brother or a sister is not under bondage in such cases: but God hath called us to peace" (1 Corinthians 7:15).***

When Job lost all he had, it was just for a season, but he got it back with more. GOD may bless you with a righteous spouse this time, but again, don't go home planning to run your spouse off. Do your best to be the righteous child of GOD that GOD has called you to be, and this will cause you to automatically be the wonderful spouse every man or woman needs. Many have come to CHRIST because of their spouse's love, and then there are many who ran for the hills of divorce. Don't let this sway you. GOD has to be first, and know that in serving HIM, your latter will be greater than your past or your former. GOD is the great transformer, so just believe HIM.

Today is a day of change. It is the day when you change the rating on your life. If you want to keep a record, purchase a calendar or a notebook and note each day's rating. Everyday, work to be better than you were yesterday. When a man's mind changes, his life automatically changes. And if that change is for the better, this is not a bad thing. Sometimes, it may look like one, but in truth, a change for GOD is a change for you. I have never seen the righteous forsaken.

YOUR PRICE

When people scan your "life tag," how much are you worth to them? How much do you sell yourself for? The less pages that are in a book, the less you're expected to sell that book for. This is how life sells itself as well. The less we've done with our lives, the less we know to expect from our lives. It is always good to know what you're selling yourself for and what you are lending yourself to.

A lot of women give themselves to men who are not their legal husbands. They engage in fornication with these men, hoping to obtain that high position of "wife" in his life. So, they give themselves away, or sell themselves at discounted rates hoping to be bought, but more often than ever, the man rents them and pays them with promises, a few meals, and a few compliments. After he's had his fill of them, he goes away, but he'll pay the full price for a woman who refuses to discount herself. He'll take her to the altar and declare himself her husband before the LORD. At the same time, many women give themselves to men who can't afford their hands in marriage. That's why you will often find a decent woman with a man who devalues and doesn't appreciate her. This is because she didn't know her value when she gave herself to him.

A lot of men discount themselves and give themselves over to situations and relationships that they are far too valuable to be

in. Have you ever seen a nice, simple man with an aggressive
and controlling woman? He's always helpful and nice, and
she's always snatching him up by the collar and going off in his
ears. You stand by wondering, "How did that happen?" He
discounted himself, and she paid and continues to pay him with
what she thinks he's worth.

Everybody in your life has already decided how much you are
worth to them. Anyone who comes into your life will scan over
you and determine how much they think you're worth. A man,
for example, will determine just how much he's willing to give
you based on how much you are willing to withhold from him.
Women often think that if they give him all of themselves that
he'd be willing to marry them, but why would he do that? Why
pay for a vehicle that you can drive every day for free? If that
man simply had to pay you a few compliments to get you, he
simply cannot value you because he's never had to really pay to
get you.

My mother told me, when I got my first car, not to let anyone
drive my car. She always said, "No one would take care of your
car like you do. They'll be careless in your car, but careful in
their own." So, I refused to hand over the keys. I'd take folks
where they wanted to go, but they weren't getting behind the
wheel. Anyhow, a lot of my friends had their vehicles crashed
when they let a relative get behind the wheel. I even rode with
a few people who were driving their sister's or their brother's
cars, and they were absolutely careless. They'd hit every hole
in the road, every animal in the way, and they didn't try to avoid
glass. Why? Because they didn't pay the price for that car,
therefore, they did not value it.

This is the same way of thinking that people have for us. When
a man or woman can get you without first having paid the price
for your hand, they simply cannot value you. It is impossible
for them to value you because they don't know what you're

worth. Even your friends will value or devalue you. You have a barcode on your life, and when people scan it, they determine how valuable you are to them. When someone has read everything they want to know about your story, or they've sold you their story, they'll simply put you back on the shelf. We can't get mad at them for doing this either because it's human nature. We get delivered from the natural man when we submerge ourselves in the WORD of GOD. If the people in your life have not been submerged in the WORD, they'll default to their human nature.

GOD priced you already, and CHRIST paid the price for you. It's up to you if you think HE priced you too high. So many of you would be so blessed if you simply refused to come from behind that glass case, and stop trying to hang out with costume jewelry. If you only paid a dollar for a necklace, why would you care if it broke to pieces? Why would you care if someone snatched it? You'd probably fall down and laugh yourself to tears if someone stole it from you. When the LORD priced you, HE wanted you to stay there. In your obedience, many of the sufferings and betrayals that you've endured would have never happened. In your obedience, only the man whom GOD has anointed for you will be able to afford you. In your obedience, only the woman who can serve as a crown to you will be placed upon your head, and you won't have child-support payments and angry ex-girlfriends. All this happened when you discounted yourself and tried to see what you could get for your good looks. You'd be amazed at how much your GOD-appointed spouse has to pay just to earn the right to take your hand. You'd be amazed at how much your GOD-appointed brothers and sisters would have to go through to earn the right to shake your hand because GOD'S children are invaluable to HIM.

However, GOD gave you a label maker, and HE allows you to sell yourself at whatever price you think you're worth. Sadly enough, the majority of people alive sell themselves for a LOT less than what they're worth. Some man comes along and sells you the idea of him becoming your husband one day. All you have to do is pay him with sex and a quiet mouth. Then, one day you look up, and he's headed down the aisle with somebody you deemed "not as pretty as you." I have heard so many women say that before, but in reality, men don't usually marry women because they are beautiful, they marry women who made them pay for their hand in marriage. And for the guys, some woman comes along and sells you the idea of her sleeping with you. All you have to do is pay her with money, cars, gifts and attention. After you've done all of this, and she gives in, you find out that you'd paid too much for that ride.

Some person comes along and wants to sell themselves as your friend, and they want to pay you with what they think you're worth. You sit there and endure the things he or she takes you through because that's what friends are for, right?
Guys: Your friend humiliates you every time women are around. To him, you are his villain, and he is winning the battle against you anytime a woman is near. In addition, he keeps getting mad at you for simple things. Today, he's mad at you because you didn't loan him that money he asked you for. Understand that you were fulfilling a role in his story, and when you went out of character, he reacted. Now, he's thinking about beating you up, and hiring someone else for your role. Ladies: What about that female friend of yours who flirts with the man you're courting every opportunity that she gets? She is always contending with you, and telling you what she thinks is wrong with you. In addition, she keeps competing and comparing herself to you. She is fulfilling her role of knocking you down to size, and you are fulfilling your role of being an ego boost for her, a giant that she has to overcome. You told these people your price, and they paid you what they thought you were worth because your price for yourself didn't match GOD'S price for you.

What should be your price? One has to fear GOD, love you, respect you, and honor the GOD in you. One has to refuse to put you inside of a box, and they have to be willing to walk away from you if GOD says they need to walk away so that HE could take you through the next season. Believe it or not, this is love. But it's so unfamiliar that people would rather have folks who stayed around them through thick and thin, blocking their blessings, and taking them out of character because this is how the world defines a friend. A friend, to most, watches them fail, and tells them what they want to hear. Personally, I would rather have a friend to tell me the truth, even if it hurts, rather than have a friend who shakes her head when I lose my footing.

GOD priced you, and HE gave you the decision to say if you stay priced at what HE requires for you, or if you'd rather sell yourself to the cutest or nicest bidder. Your story won't be worth telling if you've sold the rights to it to the devil.

FLIP THE SCRIPTURES, NOT THE SCRIPT

In our stories, there were many instances in which we had to endure situations that felt overpowering and irreparable. These situations sometimes pose as threats to life as we know it, and it is easy to become overwhelmed by the idea of defeat. Life as we know it, however, has to change as our minds change, but these changes are hard to endure when we don't have answers. Let's take, for example, the death of a loved one. Our hearts are broken by so many factors surrounding their deaths. These factors include questions, unresolved issues, unsaid words and finally, not being able to picture a life without them in it. As time goes on, the wounds begin to heal, but the scar remains. The scar is often sensitive when there are unresolved issues and questions surrounding that person's death.

We want so much to remove the things and people from our stories that take us into this realm of pain, unanswered questions and doubts. Sometimes, we just scratch them out of our stories, while other times, we look for other (illegal) ways to remove them from our stories. Important note: <u>Your enemies and your trials are essential to your destiny.</u> The real problem is not having an enemy or going through a trial; it is dealing with how you feel about the situation or the person. You may have an enemy who has hated you since the first grade, and it doesn't bother you one bit; as a matter of fact, you laugh every time you hear something else he or she has said, or every time they physically distort their faces to show you that they don't like you. Why don't they bother you? Because to you, they are too small of a problem. They don't really rank high enough because they're not on your level. Then, there are the enemies who we tend to focus much of our time and energy on because that enemy, to us, has some height or weight in our lives. That is, we either see them as a threat, or as being able to develop into a threat. Sometimes these "major threats" have dealt less heartache to us than the "low-ranking threats," but because of how we view them, we constantly find ourselves trying to deal with them or deal without them.

The script that GOD has given you to live by is embedded in you, but often we flip the script and do things "our way" because we believe "our way" produces faster results. Even though "our way" does seem to produce faster results, GOD'S way always produces final results. That's because we are temporal people, and temporal people can only produce temporary results. For example, when you use your own devices to deal with your meddling co-worker, you have to eventually come up with bigger and more evil devices to settle them down again. GOD is eternal. Therefore, any and every result that is produced by HIM is final. HE simply speaks a Word, and it is so. No devil in hell can move GOD'S Word! This is why you have to turn to the WORD of GOD to get everlasting results!

When life deals you a hard blow, and you don't know how to recover, flip the scriptures over to see what GOD told you to do. You cannot fight a devil with a devil. You can't come against anything spiritual using the natural. I know...the world has told you to flip the script, take revenge, and wear your blood-soaked clothes to demonstrate you are no one to be toyed with. The problem is anytime we take revenge; it comes back around and avenges itself against us. GOD said that vengeance is HIS. Who and what can take revenge out against GOD? Nothing and no one. When GOD told us that, it was because through HIS perfect wisdom, HE knew that life was designed to produce. We are fertile creatures and everything we send forward burrows in our lives as a seed. Meaning: When we send evil out, evil implants itself into our lives, and begins to yield fruit. Whenever you pick up a sword, the sword brandishes itself against you. So, in your flipping the script, you are simply altering the script, and causing your story to take a turn for the worse.

Pick up your Bible and read it. Don't just mark it up and kiss it from time to time, you need to read it. Learn the WORD of GOD, and learn how to use what is in the Bible to come against opposition. By staying in GOD'S will, you are causing anything and anyone who comes against you to be also coming against GOD. How crazy must they be to do that?

But we see the situation, and we see the people. We can also mentally see ways to bring the situation under submission to our will, but any and every one of our devices is designed to fail without GOD. This is to teach you that you cannot separate yourself from HIM, walk equal with HIM, or share in HIS glory, but you are to stay in your place and honor HIM through your obedience, and let HIM reign over you and your situation.

When we hear "WORD of GOD," we often think of the Biblical scriptures. This is religious thinking because in thinking of the WORD that way, we see it as nothing more than a few scribbled words on a page. The WORD of GOD is what has been spoken, and established through GOD'S mouth. So, if GOD said it, it is done. All you have to do is speak it over your situation, and the enemy has to submit himself. Satan doesn't submit to you; your words have no power over him because your breath has the stench of a sinner. We all sin; that's a given, but when you speak the words of the perfect GOD, you are standing in as a vessel of GOD, letting HIM speak through you. This is how you defeat an already defeated enemy. The devil attacked you through your sin; it is his only way in. Satan cannot touch you when you are a righteous man or woman of GOD without GOD'S permission, but when sin is found in you, you have opened up an access door for him to come in and attack you. He was standing with his foot on your neck because of your sin, but when you spoke the WORD of GOD, you placed the foot of GOD upon his neck. That's why he got up and fled.

GOD gave you the script HE has written out for you. The only thing you will find on the opposite side of the script GOD has published for you will be the script that Satan wants to publish for you. When you flip the script, you flip the script in Satan's favor! But, when you open up that Bible and flip to the scriptures, and you speak them in faith; you will cause the enemy to exit the stage. Satan loves to mess with our scripts because he has no part in the everlasting love story that GOD has written for the children of GOD.

Flip the scriptures....don't you dare flip that script! Keep doing as GOD would have you to do, even in the midst of your hurt, pain, and tragedy.

LIFE'S REVIEWS

If you have ever searched Amazon for a product and read the reviews, you'd know that the reviews of a product help or hinder its sale. You've probably taken that extra step to read the negative reviews, and click on the reviewer's name. From there, you can see the reviews that he or she has left on other products. I noticed a pattern with negative reviewers on Amazon, and any other site that allows the customers to leave reviews. Negative reviewers often give only negative reviews, or they give mostly negative reviews. This tells you a lot about the person. I don't usually trust their review of a product because I see that they have a green-thumb in planting negativity. They don't usually sow good comments because when they get a good product, to them, it's not worth reporting. Nevertheless, when a product doesn't wow them, they will take the time out to leave a long and drawn-out, negative review.

This works the same way in life. There are so many people, who if asked, would give a negative review about your life. Anyone who believes them is often just like them because negative people influence negative people; that's just the history of math. A magnet always draws after its own. Some reviewers might be right about how you "are" because they have dealt with you recently, while others may have been right in some point in history because that was how you "were."

Nevertheless, when someone attaches your past to the current you, and speaks as if you are still the same, they are in that same minute a liar. Think about a book. An author's first book is usually kind of humiliating because they make a lot of first-time author mistakes. Many try to bypass hiring an editor, and their cover designs let out a blood-curdling scream for help. As that author matures in his or her writing, their writings are better, and their books look better because they are growing up in their writing. Let's say that you went and purchased this author's first book, and you were unpleasantly greeted by bad grammar, misspelled words, and run-on sentences. Now, you see that they have a new book out, and people are commenting on it, but you want to warn them about your experience with this author's products. So, you go under their new book and add a negative review, and it reads, "I wouldn't purchase anymore books from this author. The book I purchased was poorly written, and full of grammatical errors, plus the author couldn't flow his paragraphs together. I have voted one star on this book because I am just utterly disappointed with this author's work!" Your review will have cost that author many sales because some people will believe that this is the book you are talking about. The first book is not always a reflection of what is in the current book. If the author matured, and his writing was so much better, you lied. You should have left your comment back then under the book that you purchased. You can never match a man's history to his present, unless he is presently still the way that he was.

When I was younger, I was an absolutely horrible human being. I was emotionally wounded, sick, twisted...you name it. So, I did some horrible things. I was violent, promiscuous, profane, and so on, but this is not who I am today. At that time, in my life, I was broken and trying to replace my absence of joy with its evil twin, fun. If you met any of the characters from my past, they would probably give me a bad review. Many of them know or have heard of the change that GOD made in me.

Nevertheless, many are still stuck in the past, and will never accept the current edition of a person because they are still reading the old book. Therefore, if someone said, "Tiffany is," and they connect their statement with my past, they are a liar; but if they said, "Tiffany was," and they connect their statement with my past; they may be telling the truth. When one says that you "were" a certain way, and it contrasts with how you "are" today, GOD is glorified, but when someone speaks evil of you to get others to believe that you are still the man or woman whom GOD buried long ago, they are being deceptive. But, again...only a gossip would believe a gossip because negatives draw upon its likeness.

Every review started off as a view. Someone looked at something or someone else, and reviewed what they saw. When someone views your life today, they should be able to come back and give a good review of the miraculous and unchanging hand of GOD upon your life. There will be the naysayers who, no matter how blessed you are, will go and give a bad review about you, but they can't harm you with lies when you are guarded by the truth. Understand how a lie works so that you can know how to handle it. When a word goes out, it is not a lie unless it goes against the WORD of GOD. When it goes out, it may be a spoken-word curse that has been sent to manifest itself as a fact. If that area of your life is not protected, or if a demonic access door is open in your life, that lie will make its way through that door, and manifest itself as your reality. But, when you stand on the WORD of GOD, obeying HIM, and serving HIM, HE has already declared what you are and what is allowed access to you. Therefore, when their words clash with HIS WORD, they are automatically judged as a liar. Their words come forth and strike against what HE has spoken over you, and their words are then labeled lies. Those lies then have to return to the sender and declare them a liar, and liars are already judged. That's why you see that gossips tend to have health problems. So, how do you handle a lie? By making sure it does not become your reality. You do this by staying in the will of GOD, and you can also cancel evil words sent out against you. You may ask, "How are the words evil if they aren't exactly a lie when they are sent out?" The answer is...anything that comes from a wicked heart is wicked. A bad tree cannot yield good fruit.

How you view your life will also determine how you review it. You won't always necessarily review it verbally, but you will review it through your actions. For example, a woman who views herself in a negative way will, in most cases, review her life by doing negative things to herself, like fornicating. Our choices are a mirror that reflect how we view ourselves. When a woman feels worthy of having all that GOD has promised her, she will act like it. There are many who will religiously say they are worthy of having GOD'S best, but their lives speak differently. They settle for the wrong things because they don't think they can ever get the right things. Let's take a court case where a woman slips inside of a store and breaks her hip. She goes and sues the store because the floor was wet, and the area had not been marked off. The store, after viewing the videotape of the incident determines that they are at fault, and they decide to try and settle with her out of court. She's asking $450,000 for hospital bills, time off work, and other expenses; but the store wants to give her $250,000 instead. Her lawyer will then bring this proposal to her, and she will then make a decision if the settlement amount is worth it. Now, if her lawyer feels that she could get the whole $450,000 or more, he will definitely suggest that she hold out and go for the whole amount, but if he thinks that her case isn't strong enough to get the full amount, he would recommend that she settle out of court.

You are the client, and you fell into sin. We all did. Satan attacked you and threw all kinds of accusations against you, but when you repented, GOD found you innocent. So, everything that Satan took from you is now reported as a theft. Now, Satan wants to settle out of court with you. He wants to offer you a chance to have everything you want, but first you have to drop the case against him. How you view yourself will determine what you do next. CHRIST has already told you what you're worth, and you shouldn't settle for anything less. CHRIST is your lawyer, and GOD is the Judge. The only way to get what you're worth is to stay in GOD because HE says you're worth it, and HE won't devalue you.

How we review others is a testament to how we view others, and what is in our hearts. If you find yourself seeing people in a negative way or always looking for the wrongs in a person, it is because your heart is void of understanding. This is due to the fact that you are not judging by the knowledge of what or who someone is, but you have labeled them from a prejudiced angle. People tend to prejudge what they don't understand, and this is always crippling when we don't want to understand anything different than what we know. If you find yourself always viewing people as agents of good until they have done you wrong, then it is a testament of the lack of knowledge in your heart. Why lack of knowledge? Because you obviously don't know what the WORD of GOD says about our communications, therefore, you create a false sense of knowledge wherein you determine that everyone is good, and that's what you know. But, when knowledge knocks on your understanding and presents the truth to you, then you accept the knowledge and move accordingly. In other words, you changed the truth for a lie, and accepted that lie until it bit you.

Lastly, how we handle reviews will always reflect on whether or not we believe the review has merit. For example, let's say Bill goes out and tells everyone that Bob is a convicted felon. This may agitate Bob a little, but he'll more than likely move forward if he knows that he has never been convicted of a felony. Now, if Bill was spreading this around and Bob had been convicted, you'd probably see more of a response out of Bob because what Bill is saying is true. Let's remove the example from the realm of the tangible and think of it this way: Melissa says to Jamie that she is stupid, and that her own children hate her. If what Jamie said was true, it would probably hurt Melissa more than it would make her upset, but if it wasn't true, Melissa would probably laugh it off. If it was something that Melissa is pondering in her heart, it would infuriate her because the battle within her is a tug-of-war between a lie and the truth, and she doesn't know which side to side with. Therefore, Melissa may react violently on the outside because violence is taking place on the inside. For instance, when I started off designing websites, I had a web designer that went to school for his craft, to write me on Myspace and tell me that my websites looked awful. He went on about non-schooled web designers taking the jobs from "real" web designers, and that they were putting up a bunch of junk on the Internet. That was his review of me and my work, but for some reason, his review did not hurt or offend me. I simply emailed him back and told him that I was new, and that GOD was training me. I was nice and told him I was still learning, and I ended the note with a "GOD bless you." This bothered him so much that he wrote me back to apologize, even offering to train me. He said that I could have answered him in an offensive way, and that's what he expected, but when he got the response, it made him feel awful. How I handled that review turned his heart around, and it glorified GOD. I didn't have to cut him with words; I simply cut him with kindness, and as a result; I called the blessings of GOD upon myself and reaped hot coals on his head. (*See Proverbs 22:22*) I thanked him, and didn't take up his offer because GOD was teaching me, and HE wanted to get the glory from my work. (And HE did and HE is glorified.)

Then there is the preview. A preview is a premature viewing of something. This is where so many people mess up. As human beings, we want to preview what is in store for us, so we try to sample things that should not be sampled. A movie preview is okay because it's basically a movie trailer or commercial designed to make you want to see the movie. GOD has given us a preview of what we can have, and our preview screen is called our imaginations. Our imagination can display a good preview or an evil preview. For example, most single people want to be married, and they want to know what it feels like to be a husband or a wife, so they go out and try their boyfriends and girlfriends on for size. If one is accustomed to sleeping alone, he or she would be thrilled by the thought of sharing a bed with someone. Another illegal preview usually happens in relation to our finances. It's okay to preview marriage; without the sex scenes of course, and it is okay to preview being financially stable, but it turns into sin when we try to get out and sample what we want. The reason for our wanting to sample our futures is due to a lack of patience. We want to take the cars out for test drives until we can afford to buy them. The problem with this is...you can't appreciate the new car if you're accustomed to driving it. Therefore, our previews can lead us to become impatient with GOD. You have to keep your imagination at bay, and never let it run off with your keys, otherwise you'll become anxious. You are to cast down evil imaginations, and every high thing that exalts itself against the knowledge of GOD. You're probably thinking, "How is that against the knowledge of GOD if I'm simply imagining myself in a new car, and I try to earn the money for the car?" If you've prayed for the LORD to give you a car, it is already done. Now, you are just waiting for the seasons to play out. But, here's the plot of it all: GOD knows the day, hour, and even the exact milli-second in which you will get that car. HE even knows which grains of dirt you'll be standing on when they hand you the keys. When you go out there, and start test driving the vehicle, that's okay, but when you start striving to get the vehicle, you are in the same striving against GOD because you are trusting in your own devices. Test driving the vehicle could be seen as an act of faith, but when a lack of patience comes in, we tend to respond to it by trying to reward ourselves with what we want.

The best review we can get (and the only one that counts) is the review that the LORD gives us. When HE looks at our lives, HE will respond to what we have set in motion, and what we have hindered through our motions and emotions. When GOD'S review of you is good, everything that HE has decreed for the believer is yours for the taking, but when HIS review of you is bad, everything that HE has decreed for the sinner is yours...whether you want it or not. Yes, we can repent and sometimes; the LORD will give us a lighter sentence, but the truth is...HE has already declared HIS WORD for any, and everything that we do. Whatever comes back to you is a reflection of what went out of you. If you plant an apple tree, you'd have to be three winds to the left of crazy to believe that oranges would grow from that tree. Every tree planted will yield fruit after its own kind. Send out blessings and watch blessings grow up for you.

HOW THE STORY ENDS

Most of us don't like the idea that our stories here on earth have to eventually come to an end Then again, as people grow older and older, they seem to welcome the idea of dying more and more, especially if they have made their peace with the LORD.

I remember telling people when I was younger, that I was going to party hard, and live life the way that I wanted to live, and when I got old, I'd change so I could get into Heaven. I wasn't just naïve; I was downright evil, but thank GOD for change. In my earlier life, having been raised in church, I was always afraid of dying in the state I was in. I was a sinner. I loved to party, fornicate, and contend with anyone who stepped on my feet. I trusted in my own wiles, luring men into my life with wicked motives in my heart. I knew that if I died at that time, I would go straight to hell, and this scared me. I remember consciously trying to make myself stop fornicating, but I couldn't, and I would cry about it. I felt like there was no remedy for me; I felt like I was doomed for destruction, and I didn't see anyone I could trust to turn to. So I turned to GOD, Himself, and I prayed to HIM to change me. In the beginning, I didn't see a change, but it seemed like I was getting worse. Anyhow, after I started reading the Bible everyday, and going to church often, I began to see a change, but it was subtle at first. It wasn't happening fast enough for me because I just wanted to stop sinning, but I felt like I didn't know how to do this. In truth, I just didn't know how to live righteously, so I defaulted to sin, which is what I knew. I did like many women who were caught between sin and sainthood. I started bringing my boyfriends to church. I thought that we could begin our lives as husband and wife by initiating church into our lives as boyfriend and girlfriend, but GOD said "no," to my arrangement. Everything continued to change, and I had days of absolute crying (which was, in truth, me dying to the flesh) and days of anger, but I was determined to make my end better than my beginning. I was an adult, and there was no reason for me to continue in generational curses and mindsets. There was no reason for me to continue to blame others for the turnout of my life. It was time for Tiffany to get her life in order because I have to stand before GOD for my own choices.

You have been given the right to choose how your story ends. The clock is ticking away, and one day, death is going to put a period (.) where you hoped to start a new sentence. However, this won't be your ending. There is judgment, and then there are our forever homes, and this is where our story ends or begins. In hell, the story can only end in a constant "ouch" and gnashing of teeth, and from there, there is nothing else to write about. But in Heaven, there is plenty to write about. Think of how wonderful it will be to just praise the LORD constantly. To be in HIS arms, safe from harm and feeling wrapped up in HIS love forever and ever! Knowing that no matter who loved you on earth or who didn't love you, you were always loved by HIM! It doesn't matter how you look, how much money you have, the color of your skin or how strange you are....you are loved! Imagine streets paved with gold and waterfalls flowing continuously. Imagine laughter and joy, followed by more laughter and joy. The best of it is...just being with FATHER and knowing that HE adores you! I like to joke with my friends (but I'm serious, though) about how I plan to be in HIS arms, just sucking my thumb and holding onto HIM. I will tell everyone to back off because I'm HIS baby. But in truth, HE can hold all of us at one time.

What you do in life will determine not just how your story ends, but when it ends. Sometimes sin will place a period behind us, and take us out of this world prematurely. Don't love sin because it does not love you. Let your life be one that speaks to the favor of GOD. There are so many souls who were taken from this earth prematurely, who thought that they had more time to get it right, but they didn't. And they died in their sin! They had so many paragraphs and chapters to their lives that they wanted to add to, but they never got the chance because their lives were cut short. There was a chapter, in their hearts, where they planned to change one day and do right by GOD, but everyday seemed like the wrong day because every day presented an opportunity to sin. They chose to go along with the fun and funnies of that day. Satan never tells anyone that sin's climax is death, but instead, he simply invites us to a fun-filled day, full of laughter and sin, and he tells us that we have tomorrow to get it right. He doesn't plan for us to see tomorrow; it is GOD who grants us the opportunity to wake up or not. While Satan entices the souls to sin, he then goes before the LORD to accuse them, asking for the rights to take their lives. This is evident with Job and with Peter. He asked to be able to attack Job, and to sift Peter because he was looking for the sin in them. Think about the ones whose sin he doesn't have to look for.   He simply accuses them before the LORD, reminding GOD of what HE said about the reward of the sinner. He is the accuser of man, and he wants to end your story right now.

We all wonder from time to time how our stories will end. Will we go on to glory and be rewarded for forsaking ourselves and others to please GOD, or will our last days be filled with fear because we know we did everything we wanted to do, and others wanted us to do? Don't live in sin, thinking that one day you will get it right. As I told my story earlier, one of the things that I did not mention was, I gave my life to CHRIST in my early 20s. Now, it took me a while to be delivered from those sinful ways, and generational mindsets that I'd grown accustomed to, but GOD brought me through it all, and made me all new again. I am now in my 30s, and I hate sin. I do my best to avoid it, but there are sins that we commit against GOD unknowingly, so we have to continue to pray, and ask the LORD to give us the knowledge that we need to recognize the sin, and the will and wisdom to renounce it.

I look at those elderly people who die in peace. Their families are grieving when they are sickly, but they lovingly and peacefully reach out to hold their hands to reassure them that everything will be okay. This peace comes from GOD, and this is how I want to leave this world. Not afraid, but knowing that I am going to rest in my FATHER'S bosom. You don't want to have your last days full of fear, trying to call every preacher whom you know; asking them to hurry up, come down, and baptize you in the hospital's bathtub. They end up taking too long while two sounds are scaring you dearly: the sound of the heartbeat machine, and the clock. Start your life in righteousness today because you are not promised tomorrow.

The pen is in your hand. How will your story end? You can determine how it ends by handing that pen to GOD, and asking HIM to write your story in a way that glorifies HIS name. It's not your life; it belongs to HIM. You are HIS vehicle that HE allowed to drive itself to see where it heads. The curtains one day will lower, and your story will come to an end on earth. Don't end up in hell for a few decades of fun-filled sin. It is truly not worth it! Not at all!

Review how your story began, and pay attention to how far it has come. Look at your characters, and look at your props. Look at everything and everyone around you and decide how you want your story to read before the LORD. Then ask yourself if these things or these people will alter the way that it reads. If your answer is "yes," it's time to make a change. Change is not easy for the human mind to comprehend since the mind likes repetition, but here is one amazing thing about our minds: A mind that is constantly subjected to change eventually has no problem with transition. Instead, it begins to love transition because it no longer fears it. This is when you won't find yourself getting comfortable in a certain lifestyle or environment, but you'll always be looking for the doors of change to open, and you won't be afraid to walk through them. It is true; man fears success. Man fears anything that goes outside of his limited perception. If you've been poor all of your life, you won't know what's on the other side of success, only what you perceive is there. Nevertheless, when you allow your story to continue in GOD, it won't end in failure. In GOD, your story will read on and on, and even when you leave this earth, generations will know about you because GOD will give you a good name who lives on.

Think about your children and grandchildren. Would you like to be nothing more than a story and a memory one day? Would you like to be nothing more than a picture and a few videos? A good man leaves an inheritance for his children's children. That's not just monetary, that's a legacy. You should be leaving something that touches generations for thousands of years. Can you imagine leaving teachings that bless your descendants, and others for hundreds and thousands of years, still ministering the WORD of GOD even after your departure from the earth realm?

Right now, you are working towards that day, believe it or not. Of course, this isn't your greatest peak, but it is the day that your book closes, and it is handed to the LORD. Let's make our stories are wonderful. Get rid of the villains, reassign the characters, fire some characters, and change the location of your settings. Let's give a great show, so we can have a great crowd, and let's magnify the name of the LORD in all that we do.

THE SEQUEL

What exactly is the sequel? Well, it's definitely not reincarnation, since we all know that the only reincarnation is not scriptural, so it does not happen. The sequel to your life's story usually airs through your children. They are the ones who carry on your legacy or your devils. They are the ones who will have to take what you taught them and apply it, whether it was right or wrong. That's why they are your sequel, since we can only teach what we know.

There are so many parents who try to rear their children by the motto, "Do as I say and not as I do," but we should all know by now that children rarely follow in the direction of their parents' words. Instead, children tend to follow in their parents' footsteps because these are familiar places, and they feel safe in a place their parents once walked in. Telling them to go to college, stay celibate until marriage, and to stay in church will avail you nothing if they've never seen you do these things.

Whatever giant was too big for mommy and daddy to overcome will eventually become a giant for your children. If mother can't live without a man, it makes no sense to her daughter to try to live without one either because she has been brought up to believe that a woman is only whole when a man comes into her life....or her bedroom. One of the most common situations I've run into with a lot of parents is the parent being disappointed or hurt over the choices of their children. After all, it does hurt to see one's child repeating the very same falls that once brought them down, but at this stage in the parents' life, they are saved. They have changed, and now they want to parent from where they are, but the child has learned to be who they were.

Our children will carry the torch that we give them. If that torch has no light, our children will walk in the darkness. Now, many of us came from a lineage of generational curses, and we decided to give ourselves to CHRIST, and renounce the bondage that once held us captive. Then again, many get rid of their big demons, and ignore the small ones. For example...I came from a lineage of women who don't know how to live without a man, a lineage of promiscuity, a lineage of divorce, a lineage of women molested by their relatives, and so on. So I also battled rage, hurt, and promiscuity. I got married around the age of 22 years old, and when I was cornered and couldn't figure out anything else to do to save that marriage, I filed for divorce. Not long after that divorce, I was married again. The residue of me not being able to live as a single woman was still manifesting itself, and I didn't realize it at that time. While married for the second time, problems arose, and the only solution that kept coming to my mind was divorce. I'd talked to him, pleaded with him, argued with him, and threw a few tantrums, but he was battling a generational curse himself. While mine dealt with relationships of a romantic nature, his dealt with familiar relationships. He wasn't taught that wife comes before family, and after GOD, so he battled with trying to find everyone a place of equal stature, and I wasn't having it. After many failed attempts to get him the see the light, I came to a conclusion: he's broken, and I can't fix him. So, I could divorce him, and this time, wait on GOD. I justified my way of thinking with the fact that I'd sinned my way into that marriage. Nevertheless, the LORD wouldn't let me leave because HE was delivering me, and my husband from these mindsets and curses. I renounced these things and the LORD delivered me, but I didn't know that divorce is a generational curse that trickles down generation to generation. To me, a broken man was like a broken compact disc; he needed to be cleaned up, and if he still didn't play the way I thought he should play; he was to be returned to the store or thrown away. GOD made me sit in my own pride, and it stunk worse than anything I'd ever smelled before. HE made me sit through being me, and I cried at the sight of what I'd become. I didn't know how to process hurt, even though I'd been through it a lot in my life. I was like many women today. I could deal with hurt from the family because I can just disassociate myself from them and keep on living. I could deal with betrayal from a friend because I could unfriend them in my heart and keep on living, but when it came to a marriage, I did not know how to process that pain. I couldn't just walk away. Now, on the dating scene, I had no problem walking away, but once I'd committed myself as a wife, that's when I displayed why I wasn't so good at long-term relationships. I expected people to hurt me, so I went in offensively. Once the LORD dealt with my heart, I denounced these things, and HE healed me. I am happy to say that those curses ended with me, and they will NOT be found in my children. Not in my daughters nor my sons.

I chose a different sequel, and I bless GOD for cleaning me up before I started having children. Some people had children in the midst of their sin, and these children bear the fingerprints of their mom and dad's curses.

Whatever your generational curse is, you can end it with you. Don't let that mess trickle down into your children. If you've already had children, overcome that generational curse so that they can know how to overcome it as well. I meet so many parents who get infuriated by the actions of their sons and daughters, but they themselves are still bound in that generational mindset that is on their children. Sometimes it just manifests a little differently, and this is the reason most of these parents convince themselves that the mindset did not come from them. For example, a mother who was, and is still promiscuous will be very disappointed in her promiscuous daughter. She looks at the way she was, and compares it to how her daughter is, and it's not exactly the same, so she doesn't understand that it came from her. The mother may have slept with men who gave her a girlfriend title, whereas the daughter may be casually sleeping with any man who takes her out to eat. And then there are the fathers who are hurt and disappointed that their sons aren't carrying their names to the heights of success. The dad spent his life chasing women, selling bootleg liquor, and going in and out of jail. One day, in the midst of his sin, he has a son, and this son is named after him. The son grows up, and begins to sell drugs, sleep with men, and is in and out of jail. The dad doesn't think these ways came from him since he sold liquor, and he wasn't gay. But in truth, people don't buy bootleg liquor too much anymore. People buy drugs because that's the in thing for the 20th century, and the dad was perverse when it came to women. He couldn't have enough of them, and he filled his lustful desires, whereas in his son, perversion manifested itself a different way, and he went on to fulfill his lustful desires. He is part II of his dad, whether daddy likes the sequel or not.

What's your sequel going to be like? Some of you have already begun watching it, and you don't like what's playing, but it's still not too late, even if they are adults. Children need someone to minister to them through actions, not just words. You can badger and ridicule them, but if your life doesn't mirror your words, part II is going to be a box office crash. As each generation gets worse and worse, the things of today that seemed sinfully harmless can be fatal tomorrow. This is why you need to take that first step to show your children how to get back to GOD, and how to stay there even when a storm is in their midst. Children hate hypocritical parents because they represent condemnation coming from the condemned. Could you imagine a judge sentencing you to life in prison for killing a man, and this same judge has killed 40 men in his lifetime? What a hypocrite! This is how most children see it. I've met so many women and men who are battling this today. Even women and men in my own family who lived their lives freely, but are angry to see their children falling into the same snares that once ensnared them. It would hurt anyone to consider that their children may spend an eternity in hell. No one wants this.

Your story right now will determine how your sequel plays out. Let your children say that you were strong, and you were persistent, so that they can inspire to be strong and persistent. Let them see success in you. Believe it or not, there are many people who are looking to be your sequel, even the ones who are not related to you. When I was in the world, I remember some of my young cousins (about four and five years old) would say that they were going to grow up and dress just like me because I wore the mini-skirts and the midriff tops. And of course, men were looking, but they weren't looking at me, as I thought, they were. They were looking at me as a go-cart for rent, and they wanted to see if I was worth taking a ride in. When I gave my life to CHRIST, and HE renewed my mind, HE moved all that foolishness from my heart, and delivered me from that generational curse. After my heart was changed, I wanted to re-inspire these young women who were now young adults. The hardest part was realizing that they'd have to make a choice to want to do right, but in the meantime, all I could do was live my life in a manner pleasing to GOD, and pray that one day they would want to serve HIM as well. I looked up and saw that there were many part twos to who I was, and now I want them to be part one of who GOD called them to be. At some point, all we can do is stand up, and be a template for GOD to show them how blessed they can be if they would only turn to HIM, and not to what they know.

It's up to you, however. You will make the decision as to how you want your legacy to be, and how the story begins with the children who GOD entrusted you with. You have to overcome the "I can't do it" mentality, and the "I won't do it" mentality to embrace the "GOD'S already done it" mentality. You have to just go through that struggle, and wrestle against yourself. Fight off those devils that wrote the plots and the endings for your stories. Fight off that generational mindset that set up some of the scenes that have played out for you. Take that stand today, and absolutely refuse to back down, even when the times get tough. You see; it's easy to take that stand, but what's not so easy is to stand there when the familiar is trying to seduce you back to your comfortable, sinful seats. Most people turn around and go back to what they know because it feels good to be home. Make up your mind today that you are not "most people." You can fight and overcome whatever has held you captive. Don't sit there and think that you are fully free. Sometimes people do this until they see their ways manifested in their children, and that's when they realize their way of thinking was problematic. Ask the LORD to deliver you from generational curses and any evil thing that HE sees in your heart. Sometimes, we are the ones who set up new generational curses unknowingly. When GOD starts to deliver us, HE first exposes to us just what is within the depths of our hearts. HE wants you to know and realize that you'd just been delivered. Then HE removes it. Ask HIM to build a hedge of protection around you, and to never let these demons and generational curses, as well as any demon or demonic mindsets to ever come upon you again. Work hard to stay in HIS will by praying when you feel the urge to come out of it. You have to battle yourself because you can be your greatest enemy.

What you do today will determine how your offspring's tomorrow shapes up for them. They can be so blessed, live a life that is pleasing to GOD, and pass this on to their children; or they can battle with the demons that you once embraced.

It's your choice. You are not only deciding for you, you are deciding for them. Make the right choice. Part two of me will be better than part one.

If your sequels have already begun, tear up your original script, and write a new one. Tell them about the changes, and make sure that you follow your new script. If your parents had a problem saying, "I love you" or showing any kind of affection, this doesn't mean that you have to be the same way. No, kiss your kids, hug them everyday, and tell them several times a day that you love them. That foolishness should end with you. If your sequel hasn't begun yet, tell your unborn children right now what they will not be. Then, be sure that you go on to be the very opposite of what you saw your family be. If your family is still happily acting out their evil roles, keep your children far from them. Sure, everyone wants their children to have a relationship with their families, but if my family could entice my children with hell, they need to stay far away from them. I absolutely refuse to allow sin to be acted out as if it was a good thing in front of my kids. My kids, while they are children, will never be in a house where fornication is welcomed. I choose a better sequel for them, and one day they will thank me for it. Even if they don't thank me with their mouths, they will thank me with their lives, and I will teach them to give all this glory to GOD.

Write the story and tell the truth. Because what manifests for you will manifest in part two of you, part three, four, and so on. I would hate to go before the LORD and be told that I caused my children to stumble. ***"But whoso shall offend one of these little ones which believe in me, it were better for him that a millstone were hanged about his neck, and that he were drowned in the depth of the sea" (Matthews 18:6).*** Instead, we are to teach our children how to be unapologetically blessed, and to embrace being different. Teach them not to fit in, and to know that it's okay not to fit in because children nowadays are weighed down by peer pressure. Make up your mind; I'm not raising any followers. Leaders will be birthed from my womb, and will carry on the legacy of CHRIST JESUS because that's whose legacy I am striving to carry; with HIS help, of course.

GOD'S READING

One day, we will all leave these earthly bodies, and we will stand before the Throne of GOD to be judged. Revelations tells us that JEHOVAH will open up the Book of Life, and those that are not found in it will be tossed into the pit that burns with everlasting fire and brimstone. Can you imagine the fear and dread of standing in line waiting for your time to be judged? When GOD opens up the book of life, is your story worthy enough to be listed in it or will you be on Satan's attendance roll?

Most people try to be average Christians. That is, if GOD was grading our behavior, and we could get into Heaven by living a halfway decent life, we'd make the lowest grade that we could, and barely make it in. Many would be standing by and begging for that extra point, while others would be trying to find a way to change their grades. These same people who want to be average are pretty much atheists dancing with the idea that there is a living GOD, so they hold on to the belief that HE exists, but they don't believe in HIM anymore than they believe in Santa Claus. They see GOD as a possibility because they have seen miracles that they cannot explain. They don't want to be counted out "just in case" HE is real (and we know that HE is); therefore, they go to church, read the bible (a little), and go back to living life the way that they want it. Think about it this way. Ladies, have you ever been in a relationship with a man whom you discovered was leading a double life? On one hand, he was with you and claimed to love you, but on the other hand, he's with another woman. He later explains that he was with her "just in case" it didn't work out with you. Oh and by the way, he claims that she looks just like you, so that's why she caught his eye. This is what many self-professed Christians do to GOD. They try to date the idea that HE is real, but they are cheating on what they really believe, and that is that HE is no more than the figment of our imaginations. They keep HIM around (or so they think) "just in case" HE'S real. Well, HE is. Someone with this belief system lives in sin, but visits the church. Their story reads mostly against GOD, and not for HIM, but they take the time out every now and then, to acknowledge HIM "just in case."   I remember when I used to listen to music that was demonic. During the concert, the artist; after cursing and speaking all kinds of evil, would stop for a moment and acknowledge GOD....just in case! If they believed HE was and is real, they wouldn't produce the music that they do. This is when people refer to HIM as "the man upstairs." How we refer to HIM will always show us just how we perceive HIM.

Again, imagine the stories of these characters. How are their stories reading to GOD? What about your story? We could go on and on and talk about what's wrong with the way people view GOD, and how they live the lives that are loaned to them, but it won't benefit anyone much if we don't discuss how to change the stories of our lives.

Our stories are automatically changed when our minds change. ***"And be not conformed to this world: but be transformed by the renewing of your mind, that you may prove what is that good, and acceptable, and perfect, will of God" (Romans 12:2).*** How do we change our minds, however? By taking in new information, and refusing to let old information back in. It takes prayer, and a firm decision to do what is right. Ask the LORD to deliver you from the death in you, and to keep you

from returning to the vomit that is your sin. Take the time out
to actually throw stuff away. Seriously, this is so freeing
because what you are doing is making a statement that your
life is changed from this very moment!

Old music that goes against GOD; throw it out! Clothing that
you wore in fornication, throw it out! What you are saying is
that you are no longer a part of the fornication, and anything
attached to it. Items that you were given that were linked to
romantic relationships, throw them out! Free yourself! Sure,
your mind will begin to go back and forward with itself, and
you'll hear yourself trying to reason from within. People often
say, in relation to the music they listen to, "This song isn't that
bad. I mean, most of her songs are evil, but this one just talks
about love, and the wind, so I'll only listen to this track. No, I'm
not throwing this CD out." Let's say that Satan was having a
gospel concert; would you go to it? He is wicked, and he won't
worship GOD in spirit and in truth. He'll only sing the song.
Isn't that what you are doing when you buy and listen to music
that comes from the heart of a wicked man or woman? Sure,
unlike Satan, there is hope for many of them, but until, and
unless they give themselves to CHRIST, why are you letting
them pervert your thinking? By buying their music, you have
their blood on your hands. You become one of the millions that
encourage them to stay in their lifestyles, rather than minister
a change to them. You are actually sowing a seed into the
ground that they are in, and that ground isn't holy. They are
standing in the flesh, ministering to the flesh, and you are
sowing in the flesh. You might be that one person who the
LORD uses to minister the truth to them, but because you are
sowing into their sin, you are in the same saying that what they
are doing is good. Anytime you take your blessing, and sow it
into cursed ground; you set yourself up for a cursed harvest.

Again, look around you and ask the LORD, "What is it that I
have that needs to be thrown away?" Prepare your feelings for
the hurting because HE will have you clean house, but that's a

good thing. Any time HE wants to move something out of your life, it is because HE wants to move something into your life. Get rid of those things that are hindering and keeping you from HIM. Those things aren't worth it. Anything and any person who threatens your relationship with the FATHER should not be a part of your story. Otherwise, when GOD opens up your book, HE'S going to toss it in the fire.

How do I change? How do I get my life right with the LORD? Most of us have asked that question or are currently asking that question. The answer is in John 14:5, *"If ye love me, keep my commandments."* The flesh desires to sin; that doesn't change when you get saved. You learn how to battle it, and prevent it from indulging in the very sin that wants to kill it. It is our love for GOD that will keep us, just like it is the lack of love for GOD that keeps us from HIM. When you love self more than you love GOD, you will do the desires of self. Yeah, you'll try to go back and repent, but the sin isn't just in the act itself. The sin is in the heart; therefore, repentance cannot be made by words; it is a change of the heart that takes place as a result of your love and fear for GOD. Repent means to "turn away from." It means to turn to GOD once again. Our words are a simple acknowledgment or confessing of the sin, and the acknowledgment that HE is GOD alone. Repent means to forfeit the sin and turn back to GOD. *"If my people, which are called by my name, shall humble themselves, and pray, and seek my face, and turn from their wicked ways, then will I hear from heaven, and will forgive their sin, and will heal their land" (2 Chronicles 7:14).*

You need to love the LORD enough to move past wanting to change for HIM to actually physically and mentally committing yourself to a change. Too many folks want to change, but this doesn't read well in their stories because they have been the god of their lives for so long that they have trouble getting out of GOD'S seat in their hearts. They keep trying to scoot over, hoping that they can share the Throne with HIM, and of course, HE isn't having that. Then they cry out to HIM because HE keeps telling them to throw away their sins, but they are like children gripping a piece of dirty candy; they don't want to understand that it's not good for them because it tastes so good. Why can't we just wash it off?

Think about that awful boyfriend or girlfriend that you once had. You cried and cried because you wanted that person to be the one. Why wouldn't the LORD just wash him or her off, and let you have the object of your affection? HE'S GOD. Why wouldn't HE just change them, and let you be on your way with them? Because GOD gave us free will, and GOD kidnaps no man. We have to want to change, and we have to want GOD. And then, we have to will ourselves to change, and will ourselves to accept CHRIST JESUS as our LORD and SAVIOR. Still, that's not enough because faith without works is dead. Your work is the evidence that your faith is in existence, so you have to show that you believe in GOD, and that you believe GOD. You do this through your actions. If you parked your car in an airplane hangar, would that make it an airplane? No. So why would you think that by parking your body in a church that you are automatically made righteous? Righteousness is the evidence of faith manifested.

GOD wants our books to read, "LORD, I love you! LORD, I honor you! LORD, I adore you! LORD, I worship you!" This is what our lives should be speaking to HIM. When we begin to choose to do what is right in the eyes of the LORD, we will witness HIS hand moving on our behalf. You may be saying that you love HIM from your mouth, but if what you say does not match what is in your heart, you are judged a liar. *"These people draw near unto me with their mouth, and honor me with their lips; but their heart is far from me" (Matthew 15:8).*

GOD is reading; what is your book saying? You have to forcibly change your life. A decision is hard enough to make, but what's harder is staying in place when the winds of old want to blow us back into the comforts and familiarity of sin. It starts off with a sample. We may go and hang out with a friend who is fornicating, which is sin in itself if it's not to communicate the WORD with him or her. Seeing him or her glowing, you decide to give the ex a call. The next thing you know, you're parked in sin with your headlights off, hoping the LORD won't see you. Your book has to absolutely read, "LORD; I love you." HE said if you love HIM, you are to keep HIS commandments.

The LORD requires a sacrifice. Yes, CHRIST was sacrificed for your sins, but what are you sacrificing for HIM? A sacrifice is the giving up of something that is of great importance to you. In the old law, a lamb was required for a sacrifice, but not just any lamb. You couldn't offer up a spotted, sick, lame or old lamb because that wasn't a sacrifice since people could easily give them up. GOD required a male lamb that was less than a year-old, the first of the flock. That was a sacrifice because this lamb was healthy. That lamb could have produced wool for clothing, mated, and so on.

If the LORD told you to get rid of everything tied to your fornication (which you should), but you kept that thousand-dollar necklace because you like it so much, you are still bound. Getting rid of 999 things won't avail you anything if you withhold one thing. The very thing that you find hard to get rid of is the very thing that is binding you. It's the same with relationships. The LORD may tell you to distance yourself from your old friends, and you do so, but there is one that you keep around because they have been so good to you. Can you imagine how this looks to GOD? HE has been more than good to you, yet you are more willing to hurt HIM (because you think HE'LL eventually get over it when you repent) then to hurt your friend's feelings. It is that very friend whom you can't let go of that is serving as a hindrance to your life.

A sacrifice is always the one thing you find hardest to get rid of. When the LORD required me to walk away from some of my friends, it did hurt, and it bothered me to think about how they would feel. Nevertheless, it hurt me more to be out of HIS will, so I did what HE wanted me to do. In obedience, HE explained that HE doesn't tell us to walk away only when they are a hindrance to us, but HE has us walk away when we are hindering them. We sometimes allow ourselves to be used as crutches, toilets, piggy banks, and excuses thereby adding ourselves into their books as characters that serve as substitutes to GOD. Please remember these words: "Anything that is erected as an idol must be destroyed." Don't you dare become anyone's idol.

One of the biggest sacrifices that we have to learn to make is enduring the opinions and disapprovals of others. This is hard for the average man because people don't like to offend one another. For example, I don't like to be given credit for anything. If someone says that GOD is using me mightily, or GOD is doing a great work in and through me, that's great because GOD is glorified. But if someone praises me or my work by crediting me, I don't like that. I don't want to be praised; I want the GOD in me to be acknowledged, so I often respond with "To GOD be the glory." You'd be amazed at how many people get offended when you don't accept their praise, but to accept it is to try to hold something that is not meant to be held by a man. At first, it was uncomfortable to say those words because I knew people hated to hear that. They feel as if you were correcting them, when in truth, you are protecting yourself because you don't want praise sitting on your head when the LORD for it. It does not belong to you. All praises HAVE to be given to HIM. Do you want HIM to look down from Heaven and see you standing there high on praise, and crashing into your own pride? How would you feel if you helped someone out, and they still stole from you? They had no need because you'd supplied their needs, but they still wanted your stuff, so they took it! That's how GOD sees it. We see praise as a word or words that were spoken that fade away, but praise, when it rests upon the head of a man, will pervert the man because it becomes sin in his possession. That's when you start seeing people get puffed up only to get the wind knocked out of them.

Look at the books in the Bible, especially in the book of Kings. This book of the Bible starts off telling the reader about the kings of Israel during that time. It told us whether they did what was right or what was evil in the eyes of the LORD. It also told us about the punishments that Israel endured anytime there was a wicked king. Their books are closed now, and they can't write in them anymore. We can only read what they wrote, and learn from it. Your book is still open;however, and you can change your story so that it will read that you did what was right in the eyes of the LORD. Only, to get this story, you are required to make a sacrifice. You are your sacrificial offering. You have to die to your own desires, and put on HIS will. At first, it seems like it'll be boring and hurtful. Sometimes it does seem that way when we haven't died to ourselves as of yet, but once HE takes you outside of you, and brings you into HIM; you will find that HIS plans for you are much greater than your plans for yourself. You are your own sacrifice, and you can't bring your spotted self to the altar and expect to be accepted. That is, you can't sacrifice only the things and the sins you don't care much for. You have to be willing to sacrifice any and everything that manifests as sin in your life. You have to be willing to let go of everyone who is holding you back from HIM. It doesn't matter if they are family in the natural or the spiritual; if GOD says for you to let go, you'd better let go.

You are writing your book, but it's time for you to get your book right. You can't go wrong with GOD! How your book started does not determine how your book will end. You do.

<u>RIGHT OUT</u>

"I, even I, am he that blots out your transgressions for my own sake, and will not remember your sins" (Isaiah 43:25).

Your story becomes one big mess over the course of time. One day, you're writing a great story, and the next day you've done plenty of things that you'd like the LORD to blot out. Imagine your book before the LORD, wide opened and full of errors. You want the LORD to be your editor, and clean up this great mess that you've written in your decisions; but sometimes, HE will hand your life back over to you to go into the next chapter of consequences. Sure, the LORD readily forgives us for our sins, but sometimes, we still have to endure the chastening, so we won't continue to sin against HIM. Even though the LORD forgave the Israelites, they were still punished and had to walk in the wilderness for 40 years. This is called a chastening. A chastening is when the LORD doesn't leave nor forsake the child or children, but HE punishes them. HE was still with the Israelites throughout the course of their journey and thereafter. In addition, if a woman went out and had premarital relations with a man and consequentially got pregnant, do you truly believe repentance would make the baby go away? Of course not. She'd had to carry that baby and nurture that child until he or she becomes an adult; no matter what her marital status or financial situation looks like.

The LORD indeed blessed us with HIS SON, JESUS CHRIST.

HIS blood is our "right out" for it washes away our sins and makes us new again. With HIS blood, we are able to present readable books to the LORD that aren't full of stories doomed to have bad endings. The blood of the LAMB is needed because with our sin, we would not be able to go before the LORD. JESUS not only changes how our lives read, but HE gives us a better ending by adding HIS perfection to our imperfect stories. HIS blood acts as our white out, but this doesn't mean we have the green light to sin at will. GOD said to repent and turn from your wicked ways. That does not mean to turn to sin, and then back to GOD over and over again because this is not repentance; it is outright rebellion with a hypocrite on top.

Today is a holy day. It is your day to change directions and turn your face back to GOD. Understand that sin is self-worship. We sin when we go against the LORD to serve ourselves and others. Sin is self-worship because you are serving a desire from within yourself and dishonoring the command of GOD. Adam and Eve sinned when they decided that they wanted to be like GOD, and they partook of the tree HE'D commanded them not to partake of. Sin is on a tree dangling itself for you. How many times are you going to keep picking it before you realize that behind its sweet taste is a bitter reality?

The blood of JESUS is your white-out. Today, make it a point to repent and let HIM clean up you up. After today, start each day afresh by asking the LORD to keep you from sin in that day. Dedicate each day to GOD, and get busy in your GOD-assigned role. When you're busy serving the LORD, you won't have time for sin. When you've got too much time on your hands that you are not doing anything with, you will find yourself pondering sin and eventually diving into it. You are HIS creation, and no matter what you have done, HE still loves you. Your life's choices may have been wrong all the way up until today, but now, you can choose to make it right again by choosing to do GOD'S will.

Everything that the enemy promised you was a lie. Satan will readily give you some of the things that you want, but everything that Satan gives comes with a strong after taste, and he follows up his lies with a hefty bill. He doesn't want your money or your good looks, instead, he wants you to have hell to pay. Nevertheless, what GOD gives to you will be yours, and it will continually bless you without fail.

Starting today, let's start a mental diet so that we can shed our wrong ways of thinking and gain the strength of the truth. Starting today, please do the following:

1. Pray to the LORD at least twice a day. Once when you wake up and once when you go to bed. Even when you don't feel like it, get over yourself and know that HE is worthy. Get on your knees or get on your face and pray.

2. Tell GOD what you are struggling with. HE'S already overcome it for you; all you need to do is walk in that victory. HE will lift you up out of it if you will only reach up to HIM.

3. Read your Bible daily. There will be days that you absolutely do not feel like reading the Bible, but never let your flesh tell your spirit what it is and is not going to do. Read at least one chapter a day.

4. Come together with like-minded people, and stay away from the ones that keep anchoring you in familiar thinking patterns.

5. Pray for at least one person a day; even the people that have wronged you. You'd be amazed at the power of intercession and how it will bless others, all the while coming back to bless you.

6. Forgive yourself for what you've done wrong.

7. Forgive others for what they've done wrong. Sometimes, the easiest way to forgive others is to simply start praying for them and not against them.

8. Stay away from idle speech such as gossip, complaining, slander and so on. Keep your ears clean, and your heart will thank you for it.

9. Change the type of music you listen to. This won't be easy at first because you are familiar with the singers who praise your way of thinking through song, but remember...you are embracing a whole new way of thinking, so they've got to go.

10. Pray and ask the LORD to lead you to the church building that HE has selected for you to congregate at. Don't just walk up in any church. All churches aren't GOD'S churches.

You can have a better life, but your life will not change until your mind changes. This has to be done by introducing new information to the mind, and constantly submerging the mind in this information. In addition, you have to stop opening your mind's door to wickedness through associations, music, television and so on.

Remember, this is your holy day. Mark it on your calendar and make it memorable. Then make every day memorable to GOD by serving HIM in it. When you do what's right, your book will reflect many pages where the LORD has blessed you for your right choices. HE really wants people that HE can bless beyond recognition, but many are still serving themselves, and HE doesn't bless mess.

Stand up and stand out. You don't have to be like everyone else anymore. Now, you can be like yourself as GOD has called you to be. Get up and be blessed. Today, let's right your book by removing the wrongs and recording some new rights.

If you want to change, you can. You may be craving a change, but you are afraid of what change looks and tastes like. Once you've tasted and seen that the LORD is good, you won't be afraid of change anymore; you will hunger for it more and more.

Say this prayer:

LORD, I repent for all of my sins; both known and unknown. Please cover me with the blood of JESUS; I ask that you cover my body, spirit and soul with your blood. Let your hand be upon me from on high and fill me with your precious HOLY

GHOST. FATHER, I love and adore you. Blessed is your Name forever and ever, and I ask that you continue to glorify your Name in my life. LORD, I desire to change for you. I understand that this life is not my own. I have served myself long enough, and I know that I have hurt you in the past, but today, I want to rededicate my life to you. LORD, I can't do this on my own. Please change my mind, and my life. Remove the wrong people from my life, and surround me with your sheep and shepherds. I decree and declare that JESUS CHRIST is LORD, and that HE came into the Earth in the flesh. HE was crucified, and died for our sins, and HE rose on the third day. HE lives. LORD, I ask that you bind up every demonic force, power, and principality; and cast it into the pit to await judgment. LORD, I ask that you bind every evil force that has ever attacked or attached itself to me, and never let it come back from the abyss. LORD, I ask that you close every demonic access door that is open in my life, my heart, and my mind. I ask that you seal these doors shut with the blood of JESUS. As I go through changes, I know that there will be times that I want to return to what is familiar to me, but LORD, please keep me, and never let me return to the sin and demons that once imprisoned me. Purge me with your holy fire and set warring angels to encamp around me daily, and ministering angels to minister to me daily. LORD, let your Name be continually glorified in and through me. Thank you for your love. I dedicate my life to loving you in return and displaying this love through all of my future choices.

In YESHUA CHRIST Name I pray,
Amen.

www.ingramcontent.com/pod-product-compliance
Lightning Source LLC
Chambersburg PA
CBHW031833090426
42741CB00005B/231